THE ESSENTIALS OF
SCIENCE AND LITERACY

THE ESSENTIALS OF SCIENCE AND LITERACY

A Guide for Teachers

Karen Worth, Jeff Winokur, Sally Crissman

Education Development Center, Inc.

Martha Heller-Winokur

Tufts University

with Martha Davis

Education Development Center, Inc.

Newton, MA

HEINEMANN

Portsmouth, NH

Heinemann
361 Hanover Street
Portsmouth, NH 03801–3912
www.heinemann.com

Offices and agents throughout the world

This book was prepared with the support of the National Science Foundation Grant ESI-0353368. However, any opinions, findings, conclusions, and/or recommendations herein are those of the authors and do not necessarily reflect the views of NSF.

Library of Congress Cataloging-in-Publication Data
The essentials of science and literacy : a guide for teachers / Karen Worth . . . [et al].
    p. cm.
  Includes bibliographical references.
  ISBN-13: 978-0-325-02711-1
  ISBN-10: 0-325-02711-0
  1. Science—Study and teaching (Elementary). 2. Science—Study and teaching (Middle school). 3. Language arts—Correlation with content subjects. I. Worth, Karen.
LB1585.E89 2009
372.3'5044—dc22   2009017082

Editor: Robin Manning Najar
Production editor: Lynne Costa
Cover and interior designs: Shawn Girsberger
Typesetter: Shawn Girsberger
Manufacturing: Valerie Cooper

Printed in the United States of America on acid-free paper
13   12   11   10   ML   4   5

Contents

Foreword

The twenty-first century has brought with it considerable buzz surrounding the connections between science and literacy. Everyone is looking for ways to integrate reading, writing, speaking, and listening into science lessons. But how do we do this and stay true to the process of science inquiry?

Karen Worth and her colleagues have been at the center of this discussion for more than a decade, and they share their very practical ideas and insights in the book you hold in your hand, *The Essentials of Science and Literacy*. This quartet of experts in science and literacy have grounded their work in the real classrooms of real teachers, and they suggest truly wonderful strategies you can implement immediately, as well as discuss issues that will spur you on to think about and explore the science–literacy connection more deeply.

Recognizing that many educators are more comfortable teaching literacy than they are teaching science, the authors welcome readers by focusing on the similarities (and differences) between the skills needed in science and those brought to bear in literacy. The first section of the book goes on to discuss the essential elements of inquiry-based instruction. Teachers learn to craft questions that guide and promote student thinking and discussion around a scientific concept. The next section focuses on the role of talk, first showing why students should be talking about science and then introducing explicit strategies for getting students to discuss and debate with one another rather than take part in the typical back-and-forth exchange with the teacher. The final section addresses purposeful writing about science, both in classroom science notebooks and in essays and papers meant for a broader audience.

Throughout the book teachers' voices come through loud and clear in their stories of "aha" moments, stories that demonstrate how powerful they found integrating science and literacy to be. Examples of student work demonstrate clearly what can be achieved when there is a balance between inquiry-based science and a purposeful use of language.

Another thing I like about this book is that it does not promote a particular program. Rather, the authors recognize teachers as professionals and encourage them to think critically about the role of literacy in science. Instead of providing a script or a set of steps, they present innovative ideas, thought-provoking evidence in support of these ideas, and practical strategies based on the ideas—strategies that can be immediately put into practice.

This is more than a book about integrating science and literacy; it shows how to engage students in thoughtful scientific inquiry and help them make science meaningful through purposeful talk and writing. If you are looking for ways to integrate science and literacy while making the most of the hours in the school day, you will definitely want this book on your shelf.

—*Lori Fulton*

Acknowledgments

We learned a great deal from the vision and contributions of many people while writing this book. During the development of any set of materials, there are always people behind the scenes without whom the work could not be accomplished. Here at the Education Development Center, Inc., we would like to recognize more fully the contributions of Martha Davis, who managed every detail of the work and kept us all organized, and whose thoughtful contributions to the substance of the work contributed greatly to its clarity and usefulness to a teacher audience. We also thank Kerry Ouellet for her expert and tireless editing of the manuscripts. Her persistent questioning helped to make these materials clear and accurate. And we thank Robin Moriarty, who was a member of our team when the project began and helped lay the foundation for the work.

Since the start of the project, we have worked closely with an extraordinary group of teachers: Gizelle Dizon, Amy Flax, Rachel Kramer, Suzanne Norton, and Kirsten Shrout. They opened their classrooms to us, allowing us to learn from their practice and to try out new strategies. We are deeply grateful to them.

Our work also benefitted from a group of advisors: Anne-Marie Palinscar, Betsy Rupp Fulwiler, and Wendy Saul. We thank them for their support and the time they took to offer their guidance and critique during the development of the process.

And finally we wish to acknowledge the support from the National Science Foundation, which made this effort possible.

Introduction

I knew that there were very strong links [between science and literacy]. I didn't know quite how strong, and this process of spending a year with science notebooks with my students and really trying to lift the quality of their writing as it related to the science work that they were doing really showed me how direct these links are.

—AMY FLAX, TEACHER, PERSONAL INTERVIEW

Amy Flax is a fourth-grade teacher who loves teaching literacy and science. She believes, as we do, that students need to be challenged intellectually to construct their own understanding of science, to learn how to think and reason scientifically, and she believes that talking and writing are key to that process.

But what does that really mean in the classroom? What structures and instructional strategies are needed? And, most importantly, what strategies do teachers already use from which we can draw?

This book is a result of the work we did with Amy and four other like-minded teachers. We worked together to understand more deeply what effective science instruction looks like. We realized that effective science instruction has to provide a balance of open interaction with phenomena, carefully designed hands-on experiences, and the structured and intentional use of oral and written language. We saw the benefits to student learning when they documented and recorded the work of their investigations, posed questions, and thought about and clarified their ideas. We recognized the importance of working with others, sharing and debating ideas as well as communicating with many different audiences. In other words, it was clear that oral and written communication have to be integral to all aspects of students' science learning—indeed, that there are very strong connections between science and literacy.

We know that teachers face many challenges if they want to have classrooms where the science that is taught truly reflects the practices of science, including direct experience, careful reasoning, and vigorous discussion and debate about ideas. However, if we look at science in elementary classrooms across the country, what we see rarely reflects these elements; the challenges go unmet. Among the challenges are the current emphasis on testing, a focus on literacy and mathematics, time, and teachers' own insecurities about science content. Too often the primary goal, fueled by multiple-choice tests, is coverage of information rather than deep exploration of ideas and the practice of science. In many classrooms, science is taught infrequently. In others, science instruction consists of a variety of hands-on activities about a topic without a clear conceptual focus and little to no emphasis on constructing understanding. In still other classrooms, instruction is dominated by a textbook and includes occasional demonstrations or cookbook lab exercises. Even in classrooms that use curricula with a hands-on component, that component often includes only cookbook labs, heavily structured activities designed to verify information or fun activities to motivate learning. These approaches to teaching science and these curricula provide little opportunity for students to explore a phenomenon and construct their own understanding or to experience how scientists know what they know.

In this book, we suggest, as Amy said, that while the challenges are real, instruction that emphasizes scientific reasoning and the use of talk and writing draws on skills and strategies many teachers already use as they teach literacy. They teach students discussion skills so they can discuss and debate a particular book. They guide students in the use of notebooks for their writing and reading-response journals. And many teachers instruct students in how to monitor their comprehension and actively use a variety of strategies to better understand what they are reading, such as asking questions, making connections, activating background knowledge, inferring, and synthesizing.

There are also compelling reasons to insist on a place for inquiry-based science in the elementary school program. First and foremost is, of course, the importance of science and technology in the world today and the need for an informed citizenry that can "generate and evaluate scientific evidence and explanation" and "participate productively in scientific practices and discourse" (National Research Council 2007, 2). But there are other reasons closer to the classroom:

- Science can be highly motivating, engaging students in learning and challenging them to use their intellectual abilities to understand the natural world.

- Science provides an authentic context in which students can use and develop literacy skills.

  In the science work, because it was hands-on and it was tangible, I saw the things that I wanted them to do as readers and writers happen naturally in their science notebooks and their science talk.
  —KIRSTEN SHROUT, TEACHER, PERSONAL INTERVIEW

  Science is so important to literacy because you need to write for a reason. You need to read for a reason, especially when the kids are trying to further their knowledge as they go along.
  —GIZELLE DIZON, TEACHER, PERSONAL INTERVIEW

What we are proposing in this book not only comes from what we know about classroom practice from expert practitioners but also draws support from what we know about the nature of scientific practice and the growing body of research on learning. Scientists study the natural world and attempt to explain why things are the way they are, determine how things work, and predict what will happen if . . . Children also try to make sense of the world around them. For children and scientists alike, doing science begins with direct experience with phenomena. But doing science is more than direct experience; it is a process of inquiry where understanding is constructed from experience using a creative and logical process of scientific reasoning.

There is a growing body of research that provides important new perspectives on student science learning that suggests this reexamination of how science is taught and, in particular, the development of student reasoning skills. As stated in the very important book *Ready, Set, Science!*, "Cognitive researchers have become much more sophisticated in probing children's capabilities. In the process, they have uncovered much richer stores of knowledge and reasoning skills than they expected to find in young children" (Michaels, Shouse, and Schweingruber 2007, 6). Additional research suggests that language—children's talk, their writing, and their reading—plays an important role in learning science and other subjects. And there is a small but growing research base that suggests that the reverse is also true: students' literacy skills improve when they are applied in science.

An important perspective in these chapters is that there is a common pedagogical basis to an inquiry-based approach to science teaching and a balanced approach to literacy teaching. It comes from current research in learning that points to the importance of actively engaging students in their learning and challenging them to think, reason, and take responsibility for that learning. It is this common basis that makes possible many connections between science and literacy instruction in the classroom.

> *I found that when they were working in science, they'd sit around a table and be working on an activity or observing what was happening as they were putting batteries and bulbs together, and those conversations would naturally come up. It was interesting to sometimes just sit back and watch the kids talking. I'd say to myself, "Oh, we worked on that in reading and here they're doing it just naturally around the table." It wasn't something that I had to teach a lot during science.*
> —KIRSTEN SHROUT, TEACHER, PERSONAL INTERVIEW

This book focuses on the role and use of talk and writing in science. This is not to suggest that reading is unimportant in science; on the contrary, scientists spend many hours reading about the subject of their research. They build on the ideas of others as well as devise ways to challenge them. Students do need to learn to read critically. They need to gather information and compare their ideas with those of others. They need to learn how others have gone about their work and to experience the ways in which the natural world is described in literature. However, we have not addressed reading here because the use of books in science instruction has been discussed by many educators (see "For Further Reading" at the end of Chapter 2, "Balanced Literacy and Science Inquiry"). In addition, elementary teachers are more comfortable with the use of books than they are with writing and talk in science. And finally, the role of books in the development of scientific reasoning skills is less critical than that of writing and talk.

Nor do these chapters cover all the talk and writing that takes place in the science classroom. Small-group discussions, for example, are not emphasized nor are the rich class discussions about planning and designing investigations. We hope you will go beyond what is here and think about these and many other connections between science and literacy that can be implemented in the classroom. This book is written for the upper elementary years, but teachers of younger children will find much that is relevant to their work.

There are three sections in the book: Essentials, The Role of Talk in Science Inquiry, and Writing in Science. Each section has a brief introduction followed by two to four chapters. Each chapter concludes with a number of items for further reading. The chapters are not intended to be read in any particular order. You are encouraged to browse through them, selecting the ones that catch your interest. Each chapter is an invitation to try new strategies in the classroom and a provocation for further thought. And above all, the chapters are written to encourage teachers to provide students with rich and challenging experiences in learning science.

Readers of this book may choose to simply read and reflect on what is here. We hope that many others will choose to work in a group discussing the ideas we have presented and sharing their classroom practice. To support such teacher groups, we have included a study guide at the end of the book with suggested structures for working together, as well as a list of questions for each section and chapter that may provide a focused starting point.

SECTION ONE

Essentials

The science- and literacy-instruction connections described in this book are connections between a particular instructional approach to science and a particular instructional approach to literacy that share a common perspective on how children learn, on what kinds of classrooms effective learning takes place in, and on specific strategies that support that learning. Therefore, the first two chapters in this section describe these approaches: inquiry-based science and balanced literacy.

The two approaches are based on a common understanding of student learning, the role of the teacher, and the nature of the expectations of a classroom culture that supports this learning. Both view learning as constructed by the student and guided by a teacher using a balance of direct and guided instruction. Both seek to challenge students to take on growing responsibility for their own learning as they develop new skills and strategies. At the core of both approaches lies a challenging reasoning process. In each, students talk, write, and read to better understand a text or a phenomenon; they then take on the challenge of communicating their understanding to a larger audience. Both approaches emphasize the role of formative assessment and the adaptation of instruction to meet students' needs. The classroom norms and expectations needed for both inquiry-based science and balanced-literacy instruction guide students to respect one another's ideas, cooperate and collaborate with one another, take risks and ask questions, and assume responsibility for their learning.

Talk and writing are fundamental to learning in both science and literacy. In both domains, encouraging students to talk is key. Although the nature and substance of the talk are different, the basic skills, norms, and expectations are the same and can be taught and used in both science and language arts. Students learn writing skills in literacy class, and science provides an authentic context in which to develop and practice them. One purpose of writing common to both literacy and science is to record, review, and reconsider ideas and questions. Another is to communicate ideas to a broader audience, whether about a science idea or a literacy challenge.

While there are many connections between what is taught and learned in literacy and in science, it is important to make explicit the differences as well as the similarities between the skills learned in literacy and those used in science. This can help students deepen their understanding of how they think and reason in each domain as well as apply their learning across domains. Notebooks, for example, have different purposes and structures in science and literacy. These are elaborated in Chapter 7, "The Science Notebook."

The first two chapters, "Science Inquiry" and "Balanced Literacy and Science Inquiry," describe classrooms in which teachers are successfully engaging students in science inquiry with a strong emphasis on literacy. In such classrooms, the following characteristics are fundamental.

- Direct investigation of phenomena is at the core of student work.

- Collaborative and cooperative work is the norm.

- Student-to-student talk is explicitly taught, and basic norms and expectations of interaction are known and accepted.

- Small- and whole-group discussions occur regularly, with an emphasis on comparing data and sharing claims, evidence, ideas, and explanations. Debate and the use of evidence are ongoing.

- Students keep structured science notebooks that detail the unit of study and its component investigations, as well as student reasoning, ideas, and questions.

- A variety of books and technological resources supplement, support, and enrich direct investigation but do not substitute for it.

- Direct instruction, careful facilitation, and modeling of skills and thinking guide student learning.

- Students gradually assume more and more responsibility for their learning.

Chapter 3, "Teacher Questions That Support Inquiry," discusses how carefully structured questions are key to initiating an investigation, prompting a productive discussion, and guiding students' reasoning. Because questions are so important to both literacy and science and also difficult to frame, this instructional strategy is singled out and discussed in its own chapter.

The first section concludes with "Science Inquiry and English Language Learners," which highlights instructional strategies that are particularly supportive of English language learners, a growing population in schools. This is of particular importance because evidence suggests that science instruction that balances both direct experience and time for talk and writing can provide rich opportunities for English language learners not only to learn science but also to develop their English language proficiency and communication skills. These same strategies also can be helpful for non–English language learners whose language experience is less rich than others'.

CHAPTER 1 | **Science Inquiry**

Inquiry is a multifaceted activity that involves making observations; posing questions; examining books and other sources of information to see what is already known; planning and conducting investigations; reviewing what is already known in light of experimental evidence; using tools to gather, analyze, and interpret data; proposing answers, explanations, and predictions; and communicating results.

—NATIONAL RESEARCH COUNCIL, *NATIONAL SCIENCE EDUCATION STANDARDS*

A recent publication of the National Research Council titled *Taking Science to School: Learning and Teaching in Grades K–8* (2007) identifies four goals of science education. The authors state that to be proficient in science, students must

- "know, use, and interpret scientific explanations of the natural world;

- generate and evaluate scientific evidence and explanations;

- understand the nature and development of scientific knowledge; and

- participate productively in scientific practices and discourse" (2).

Similar to many such documents, these goals include knowledge of scientific explanations of the natural world and an understanding of how scientific knowledge is generated. But these four goals also place strong emphasis on the importance of teaching students to develop their abilities to reason scientifically and engage in scientific discussions. The goals reflect the growing understanding that it is not enough for students to have hands-on experiences if they do not reason about what they have done, develop claims backed by evidence, and try to explain what they have found out.

So what are the implications for teaching science in upper-elementary classrooms? Over the past twenty years, educational research has revealed a great deal about what is important for learning science. There is broad agreement that students must engage in the hands-on investigation of phenomena. But to really understand how scientific knowledge is developed and how it is practiced, as well as to develop a deep understanding of important concepts, students also need to learn to reason about their experiences. They need to talk and write about their ideas, listen to the ideas of others, and read about science using print, the Internet, and other resources critically. Given these goals for science education and the research about learning, it is clear that literacy is an integral part of science learning and that learning science happens through a process of scientific inquiry.

▶ Teaching and Learning Science: An Inquiry-Based Approach

This chapter describes an approach to teaching and learning science based on inquiry and guided by current research and the goals of *Taking Science to School*. To highlight important elements of this approach, three classrooms, all studying insects, their basic needs, and their life cycles, are compared using the Inquiry Learning Cycle.

Introducing the Classrooms

In classroom A, the teacher provided a number of trade books about insects that complemented the text chapter on life cycles. Over several weeks, students read two of the books, used the Internet to research life cycles of at least three other insects, and then wrote a research report on the topic. This unit culminated in the written reports.

The teacher in classroom B provided live painted lady caterpillars. Students observed the caterpillars over four weeks, making regular drawings and notes in their science notebooks as the insects developed from larvae to pupae to adults. The teacher also made available books about butterflies and provided time for students to read these books about insect life cycles. The unit culminated with the release of the adult butterflies.

Classroom C reflected the inquiry-based approach. The teacher provided live painted lady caterpillars and mealworms, allowing students to observe the metamorphic life cycles of two different organisms. Students drew and made notes regularly in their notebooks and the teacher provided books and other resources. But in addition to this, the teacher planned small- and large-group discussions and times for writing in which students thought deeply about what they were seeing, raised questions, and shared and debated ideas. Students discussed questions such as *What are you noticing? What questions about life cycles have been raised by your observations? What are your ideas about life cycles at this point in our investigation?* The unit culminated in a class discussion and class book about how the life cycles of different kinds of insects are the same and different and how an insect life cycle compares with the life cycle of a familiar mammal.

The Inquiry Learning Cycle and the Three Classrooms

Figure 1 is a diagram of the Inquiry Learning Cycle, which has four basic stages. The stages are shown as sequential, but the arrows suggest that the process of inquiry is not linear, and students will often return to an earlier stage as they investigate a concept.

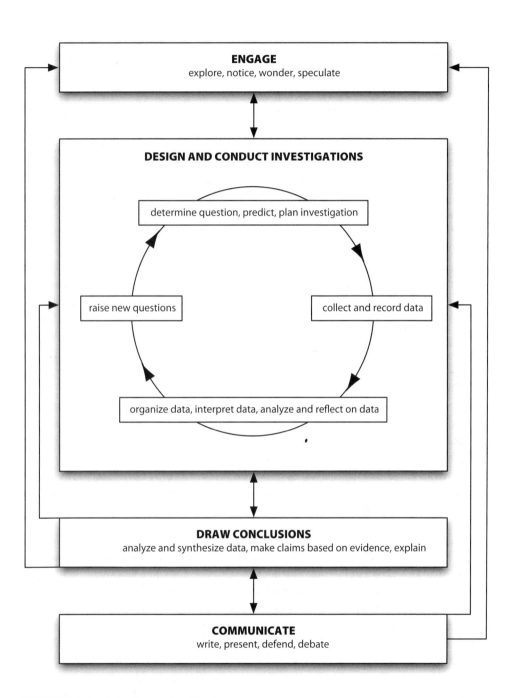

FIGURE 1 Inquiry Learning Cycle

Stage 1: Engage

When beginning a scientific inquiry, students need to become familiar with the phenomenon at hand and become aware of the ideas and knowledge on this topic that they bring from their prior experience. During the first stage of inquiry, the Engage phase, students use materials to explore a phenomenon, and they talk and write about their ideas, experiences, questions, and interests. During this stage, open-ended explorations and gathering-ideas discussions provoke curiosity, elicit prior knowledge, and build motivation for further investigation. The teacher carefully identifies the basic concepts to be addressed and plans the Engage stage in such a way that student explorations and discussions, while open-ended, relate closely to the critical concepts to be learned. At this stage, the teacher must resist the urge to deliver information or correct students' thinking.

The teachers in classrooms A, B, and C all provided opportunities for students to reflect on their prior experiences before they began their investigations. In classroom A, students created a class chart that listed things they knew about insects, their own experiences, and questions they had. Such an activity can encourage students to share wide-ranging ideas and experiences. It is more of a brainstorm than a focused reflection. In classroom B, the students created a similar chart but had real caterpillars on hand to prompt their thinking. Having the actual organism both focuses student responses and provides students who have less experience or are English language learners with something concrete to ground their thinking.

In classroom C, the teacher focused the students more closely on the science concepts to be studied. She gathered the class in a discussion circle, introduced a live caterpillar, and asked, "Yesterday I found this insect in my backyard; what do you think I need to do to keep it alive and healthy?" Then she asked, "What do you think will happen to it?" The carefully crafted questions focused the students' responses on the basic concepts of needs and life cycle and asked them to draw from their knowledge and experience to respond.

Stage 2: Design and Conduct Investigations

The Engage stage of inquiry provides all students with a foundation for pursuing investigations in greater depth. During the second stage, called Design and Conduct Investigations, the teacher guides students as they investigate particular aspects of the phenomenon under study—aspects that will lead them to better understand the selected concepts. The process begins with clarifying the question to be addressed. The question may come directly from the curriculum, may be determined by the teacher, or may originate with the students. In any case, students should understand and be able to articulate the question. Once the question is stated, either the teacher or the students provide a procedure for the investigation. Regardless of where the procedure originates, the students think, talk, and write about how best to pursue the question and what they predict may happen. The teacher scaffolds and guides the discussion as needed, ensuring that all students understand the nature of the particular procedure and why they are using it. This stage also includes collecting data through observation; organizing and recording data in charts, graphs, descriptions, drawings, or diagrams; and, finally, beginning to interpret and analyze the data.

While designing and conducting an investigation, students carefully document in their notebooks what is going on as the investigation unfolds as well as ideas, questions, and their growing understanding. They participate in small- and large-group discussions to share, debate, and reflect on ideas. The teacher guides their inquiry and discussion as needed, gradually moving students toward greater independence in their work.

Students in classroom A learned about insect life cycles secondhand by reading and looking at pictures from books and the Internet, talking about the information, and reporting their findings in a written report. These students were exposed to correct information and vocabulary use. They saw photographs and descriptions of insects going through the life cycle. Without investigating actual insects, however, their sense of time and scale could have been inaccurate and they might have been less likely to internalize and remember the concepts. Without participating in the process of inquiry, these students were unlikely to increase their understanding of the nature of science and how scientists learn about the natural world. Aware of this, their teacher encouraged students to wonder how the person who wrote or illustrated the book might have obtained his information, in what ways real-life insects might differ from the ones depicted in the books, and what they would need to do to write a book about the life cycle of an insect they found in their school yard. In the end, however, the students did not engage in planning and implementing an investigation nor did they collect their own data.

The teacher in classroom B engaged students by providing live insects to observe. However, with only one species of insect there was little opportunity to collect data that might lead to a more general understanding of insects and the important stages of metamorphosis.

The teacher in classroom C combined more complex direct experience with the use of print and other media, writing, discussion, and presentation to address both students' conceptual understanding of life cycles and their understanding of how science knowledge is developed. Having two species to compare and including discussions, writings, and questions sharpened students' observations and encouraged them to reflect on how their ideas about life cycles may have been changing as a result of new evidence—evidence that included direct observations, comparisons, their peers' perspectives, and secondary resources.

Stage 3: Draw Conclusions
With significant investigations completed, the inquiry moves to the next stage. To draw conclusions, students revisit their investigation question and predictions and

review their notebook entries with special attention to their data. Before developing their conclusions, students review their thinking and debate their ideas in small- and whole-group making-meaning discussions. Finally, they prepare a written conclusion: they state their claim, providing evidence from their data to back the claim, and, in a separate step, they may try to explain an outcome, speculating on why something happens the way it does.

In classroom C, working in small groups, students reviewed their notebook entries, including reflections, and agreed upon what claims about insect needs and life cycles they thought their data could support. In the whole group, students discussed and debated these claims and proposed possible explanations for variations in the two life cycles they observed.

In classrooms A and B, this important stage was basically missing. Without an opportunity to draw conclusions from their observations, students in classroom B missed a chance to hone their reasoning and thinking skills and to better understand how science works. In classroom A, as part of writing their reports, the teacher encouraged her students to think about how scientific information makes its way into books and whether the sources used were always in agreement. By doing so, she encouraged students to think about how others might have come to their conclusions, but the students did not experience the process themselves.

Stage 4: Communicate

The final stage is Communicate. When students finish a unit of study (or perhaps when they are partway through and have something to share), they present their discoveries to a wider audience. The audience may consist of classmates, other classes, the school, or the wider community. Students may participate in a poster session or debate, write an article for the school paper, or write a letter to a local politician or business.

The teacher in classroom B used the release of the butterflies as a culminating experience but did not ask the students to come to closure on their thinking and learning about insects. In classroom A, students wrote insect reports based only on secondhand experience from books and the Internet. In classroom C, students had an opportunity to come together as a class, synthesize what they had learned from their direct experiences, and create a book based on their direct experiences with inquiry for others to read.

▶ Conclusion

Classroom C is a snapshot of a classroom that reflects an inquiry-based approach to learning and teaching. Inquiry-based science has at its core active firsthand engagement with materials and objects from the natural world. But equally important is a challenging reasoning process in which students share, debate, argue, write about their work, and read what others have said and done. Books and other sources of information and inspiration play a role as well, supplementing and enriching the direct experience.

These varied experiences lead to a deeper understanding both of the concepts that underpin the investigations and of the nature of the scientific endeavor. In classroom C, science investigations don't just incorporate literacy skills; the use of literacy skills is *required* at every stage.

▶ For Further Reading

Donovan, Suzanne M., and John D. Bransford, eds. 2005. *How Students Learn: Science in the Classroom*. Committee on How People Learn. Washington, DC: National Academies Press.

This book, published several years before *Taking Science to School* (Duschl, Schweingruber, and Shouse 2007), applies the findings from *How People Learn* (Bransford, Brown, and Cocking 1999) to K–12 science instruction. The book is a practical interpretation of *How People Learn* and includes examples of strategies for classroom instruction.

Duschl, Richard A., Heidi A. Schweingruber, and Andrew W. Shouse, eds. 2007. *Taking Science to School: Learning and Teaching Science in Grades K–8*. Washington, DC: National Academies Press.

This report addresses the goals of science instruction and synthesizes recent research on science teaching and learning. Basing their work on the research and a new definition of science literacy, the authors present a framework for what it means for students to be proficient in science and offer some recommendations for how to achieve these proficiencies in educational settings.

Hackling, Mark, Shelley Peers, and Vaughan Prain. 2007. "Primary Connections: Reforming Science Teaching in Australian Primary Schools." *Teaching Science* 53 (3): 12–16.

This article describes Primary Connections, a professional development program with accompanying curriculum units for both preservice and inservice teachers. The program is inquiry based, uses a 5E teaching model, embeds assessments into teaching and learning, encourages cooperative learning, and links science and literacy. The authors also report on research and discuss the positive impact the program has had on teachers' confidence and practice, students' science learning, and the overall importance of science in the schools.

Hammer, David, and Emily van Zee. 2006. *Seeing the Science in Children's Thinking: Case Studies of Student Inquiry in Physical Science*. Portsmouth, NH: Heinemann.

This program presents written and video classroom vignettes from grades 1 through 8 that are intended to help practitioners look for evidence of student science understanding. The authors support the readers and viewers by providing background about how students at these ages learn science and engage in investigation. There are also detailed facilitator's notes for running effective staff development workshops.

Harlen, Wynne. 2001. *Primary Science: Taking the Plunge.* 2d ed. Portsmouth, NH: Heinemann.

This book makes the case for inquiry-based science and explains and describes a range of implementation strategies. It addresses directly how literacy is central to inquiry-based science teaching. The chapters "The Right Question at the Right Time" and "Helping Children to Communicate" pay particular attention to the connection between science and literacy.

Michaels, Sarah, Andrew W. Shouse, and Heidi A. Schweingruber. 2008. *Ready, Set, Science! Putting Research to Work in K–8 Science Classrooms.* Washington, DC: National Academies Press.

This book is a companion to *Taking Science to School*, the report produced by the Committee on Science Learning, Kindergarten Through Eighth Grade of the National Research Council. It is written for practitioners, presenting the findings from research and implications for instruction. Detailed classroom vignettes illustrate many of the observations and conclusions about science teaching presented in the original report.

CHAPTER 2

Balanced Literacy and Science Inquiry

If you're thinking to yourself, "Well, I can't teach science. This is too challenging. This is too different," it's really not that different [from teaching literacy]. I've been amazed by the links between literacy skills and science. We just don't think of it that way. One thing I think of are the different kinds of conversations that we have in our literacy work. It's a very powerful tool for developing comprehension skills, for developing conversation, and [for] being able to synthesize what we're thinking about as we read. And, it's only a little different with our discussions about our science investigations.

—AMY FLAX, TEACHER, PERSONAL INTERVIEW

Balanced literacy is an approach to reading and writing instruction based on current theory and research. It includes explicit instruction in skills and strategies taught through whole-class mini-lessons, small-group work, and individual conferences.

Balanced literacy has its roots in constructivist teaching and emphasizes opportunities for children to actively engage in the learning process. In addition to direct instruction and explicit modeling, teachers provide many opportunities for students to practice reading and writing strategies on their own, first with close guidance from the teacher and then independently. Essential within a balanced-literacy approach is the assumption that students will develop responsibility for and independence in their work, whether in whole-group settings, small groups, or individually.

Just as the approach to inquiry science emphasizes helping students develop their ability to reason, debate, and communicate their ideas, balanced literacy takes a similar approach to the teaching of writing and reading. This chapter explores key elements of balanced literacy and how they connect to inquiry-based science.

▶ Talk in a Balanced-Literacy Classroom

As in inquiry-based science, the role of talk in a balanced-literacy classroom is quite different from its role in the more traditional classroom, in which teacher talk dominates. In balanced literacy, student talk is seen as fundamental to literacy learning. Students learn to share their ideas with others and have those ideas considered, challenged, and revised. As students talk about text and ideas with one another before, during, and after reading, their comprehension improves. Talk also is a rehearsal for writing as students articulate thoughts and ideas out loud prior to committing them to paper.

Time for talk is provided throughout literacy instruction as well as through the use of three common structures: literature circles, shared reading, and interactive read-aloud. During literature circles students come together in small groups to discuss a particular book; they engage in meaningful and purposeful peer-to-peer discussions about a text, similar to the conversations of an adult book club. Students provide evidence from the text to support their thinking and engage in respectful debate. Students are likely to refer back to their reader's notebooks or reading-response journals, in which they have recorded questions, thoughts, observations, reflections, and reactions to the text while reading. This is not dissimilar to the discussions students have as they conduct and reflect on their science investigations.

Talk also plays a central role during shared reading, when the teacher reads aloud an engaging piece of text, modeling fluent reading while students read along silently. Students either have copies of the text in hand or view enlarged text on an overhead. As the teacher reads a nonfiction text, she might stop and focus on a specific structure used in the text such as question and answer or cause and effect. Shared reading always includes explicit instruction. The teacher pauses periodically to think aloud, modeling how a proficient reader integrates comprehension strategies to make sense of the text, uses strategies to decode and uncover the meaning of unfamiliar words, and makes use of text features and text structures. She might also read a bit of text and think aloud so as to model how one might sort important ideas or identify key ideas that support a particular concept students are learning. Such modeling using explicit language can highlight the possible ways that a student might interact with a piece of text independently.

During an interactive read-aloud, the teacher reads aloud a piece of high-quality fiction or nonfiction writing to the whole class and stops at planned spots to ask questions that elicit student responses. Students learn to think deeply about text, to listen to others, and to grow their own ideas. Interacting and debating ideas are expected after explicit modeling has been provided. As students discuss the question or idea posed, the teacher encourages them to linger, react, provide evidence for their thinking, and talk directly to each other rather than engage with her in a more traditional call-and-response exchange. These discussion skills are quite similar to those students need when discussing their science work.

▶ Writing in a Balanced-Literacy Classroom

When teaching writing in a balanced-literacy classroom, teachers immerse students in books and other types of texts they might use as models for later writing. In addition to learning about genres, students consider the audience and purposes for each type of writing. When students are introduced to a new unit of study in writing, they gather entries in their writer's notebooks.

Ralph Fletcher (1996) refers to a writer's notebook as an "incubator": a place to hold ideas for future writing. Although a science notebook has a different purpose and structure, it too is used as a source of information when students use the work they have recorded in their notebooks to craft longer pieces of writing. During writing in science and in literacy, once they embark on the actual writing, students draft, revise, edit, publish, and then celebrate their work. Explicit instruction should be provided by the teacher throughout the writing process, based on student needs. This cycle is the same regardless of the discipline. But again, there are differences to highlight. For example, in science, if observation, diagrams, and labeled drawings are included, they are as objective and specific as possible; on the other hand, in literacy, observations in words and images may be more subjective.

◗ Development of Thinking Skills in a Balanced-Literacy Classroom

In addition to teaching students to become strong readers and writers, a balanced-literacy approach values thinking. Students learn to monitor their comprehension and to actively use a variety of strategies to better understand what they are reading. Proficient readers use an array of strategies to make meaning from text. Teachers model these strategies, including how readers ask questions, make connections, create sensory images, activate background knowledge, determine importance, draw inferences, and synthesize (Pearson et al. 1992; Zimmermann and Keene 2007). As they progress as readers, students learn to integrate these strategies and apply them to increasingly complex and varied forms of text.

Scientific reasoning also is a meaning-making process focused on understanding scientific concepts. When students reason scientifically, they use many of the same strategies although in slightly different ways. Predicting is one example. When students predict in reading, the prediction is based on their interpretation of the author's intention. In science, a prediction is based on the student's prior experience and knowledge of a natural phenomenon. Inferring is another example. In literacy, inferences are based on a combination of what a student reads and her prior knowledge or schema. An inference is something that is probably true. In science, inferences are based on observations and data. Inferences or claims are made using experimental data as evidence rather than citations from a text. Making explicit the links—the similarities and the differences—between the strategies learned in literacy and those used in science can help students deepen their understanding of their own thinking as well as connect their learning across subject-matter domains.

◗ Conclusion

This description of balanced literacy suggests that many of the skills students need for talking, writing, and reading in inquiry-based science are taught within a balanced-literacy approach. It also underlines how inquiry-based science and balanced-literacy instruction take a common approach to student learning. At the core of both approaches lies a challenging reasoning process. Students talk, write, and read to better understand a text or an investigation and then take on the challenge of communicating their understanding to a larger audience.

Just as science writing and reading can be done as part of literacy instruction, student literacy skills can be reinforced in the authentic context of inquiry-based science. In classrooms where time is at a premium, especially for science, this relationship can lead to more time for science investigations.

For Further Reading

Calkins, Lucy M. 2001. *The Art of Teaching Reading.* Boston: Allyn and Bacon.

> This comprehensive book about reading instruction includes a number of chapters that have implications for how to connect science and literacy. In particular, the chapter "A Curriculum of Talk" offers many ideas and strategies applicable to the role of talk in science teaching.

Cazden, Courtney B. 2001. *Classroom Discourse: The Language of Teaching and Learning.* 2d ed. Portsmouth, NH: Heinemann.

> In this book, Cazden revisits her classic text (1st edition, 1988) and integrates current perspectives and research. The book makes a strong case for the value of student-teacher talk and the importance of oral communication in current conceptions of how students acquire knowledge.

Graves, Donald H. 1989. *Investigate Nonfiction.* Portsmouth, NH: Heinemann.

> This book makes a strong case for how discourse connects with reading and writing as students explore nonfiction text. Students talk about real events and phenomena they encounter as they examine the world. They are motivated to extend their understanding as they read for information, record data, and write about what they are learning.

Harvey, Stephanie. 1998. *Nonfiction Matters.* Portland, ME: Stenhouse.

> This book presents practical strategies teachers can use as they introduce the skills and strategies students need to grapple with the complexity of reading and writing nonfiction. The book includes examples of student work, two-column notes, and other scaffolding templates that can be used by teachers in classrooms. The author clearly states the importance of voice in nonfiction writing and also encourages students to research their passions and develop other skills that enable them to become independent thinkers.

Palinscar, Annemarie Sullivan, and Shirley J. Magnusson. 2001. "The Interplay of Firsthand and Text-Based Investigations to Model and Support the Development of Scientific Knowledge and Reasoning." In *Cognition and Instruction: Twenty-five Years of Progress*, ed. Sharon M. Carver and David Klahr, 151–94. Mahwah, NJ: Lawrence Erlbaum.

This chapter describes the development of a research program on the use of text during guided inquiry instruction. The authors discuss an initial study of an expert teacher who incorporated text into her inquiry instruction—which informed the development of a new text genre modeled after a scientist's notebook—and then proceed to a discussion of a study comparing the new genre with a more traditional text. The authors found that the new text genre, which models the use of scientific reasoning, provided more opportunities for students to reflect on and respond to their reading.

Saul, Wendy, and Sybille A. Jagusch, eds. 1991. *Vital Connections: Children, Science and Books*. Portsmouth, NH: Heinemann.

The editors of *Vital Connections* have gathered brief papers written by prominent children's authors, children's books critics, teachers, and others to go beyond the simple use of books for specific information and to consider the more complex roles books can play in bringing children and science together.

Topping, Donna H., and Roberta A. McManus. 2002. *Real Reading, Real Writing: Content Area Strategies*. Portsmouth, NH: Heinemann.

This book is a practical approach to supporting the teaching of reading and writing in content areas, with a particular focus on science. The authors, one a middle-level science teacher, the other a literacy professor, recount their twenty-three-year collaboration to find ways to get students to deepen learning in the content areas.

CHAPTER 3 | Teacher Questions That Support Inquiry

A good question is the first step towards an answer; is a problem to which there is a solution. A good question is a stimulating question, which is an invitation to a closer look, a new experiment or a fresh exercise. The right question leads to where the answer can be found: to the real objects or events under study, there where the solution lies hidden. The right question asks children to show rather than to say the answer: they can go and make sure for themselves. I would like to call such questions "productive" questions because they stimulate productive activity.

—JOS ELSTGEEST, "THE RIGHT QUESTION AT THE RIGHT TIME"

Science is all about questions; scientists' work is to ask and seek answers to questions about the natural world. The idea of a question as an invitation is in character with the inquiry-based approach to teaching and learning.

Visit a typical classroom and listen to what the teacher says during a science lesson. A good part of the time, he is asking questions, all kinds of questions:

- Is your science notebook open to yesterday's data chart?

- Did you remember to put the date and a heading on the top of the page?

- What did you find when you measured your plant?

- What does your data tell you about the effect of light on plant growth?

- Based on your graph, what can you say about the strength of magnets?

Some of these questions are routine reminders phrased as questions: *Did you remember to put the date and a heading on the top of the page?* Some ask for specific information: *Has your plant grown taller this week?* Other questions have a different purpose: to stimulate scientific thinking.

Questions are a teacher's stock-in-trade and can be powerful tools for focusing and guiding students' learning during science inquiry. Crafting just the right question requires hard work and thoughtful planning. A short, straightforward question that initiates a lively and complex discussion or interesting piece of writing during a science investigation can sound disarmingly simple but likely results from a great deal of thought. While this chapter addresses teacher questions, it is important to note that the development of *students'* ability to ask good questions is also a goal in inquiry learning.

The role of the investigation question is really critical. Making sure you have a good question is something that is certainly worth putting effort into. I approach it the same way I approach literacy work that we do, which is that I want to come up with a really clear question. I want to post it. A question has to be accessible and available to the entire community. And I think in the case of a question that is going to guide an inquiry, guide the work that they do, you want to be really clear. You want to be really focused. You want the kids to be thinking, thinking, thinking in their minds about that question over and over again.

—AMY FLAX, TEACHER, PERSONAL INTERVIEW

▶ Questions and the Inquiry Learning Cycle

The Inquiry Learning Cycle described in the first chapter reflects the practice of scientific inquiry. Questions help students know what learning steps to take at each stage of inquiry. In the first stage (Engage), students are introduced to a new unit or investigation; here the purpose of the question is to invite students to grab hold of their own ideas and experiences with the topic, to become intrigued, to wonder, speculate, and explore. Once students are engaged, teachers move to the Design and Conduct Investigations stage, asking questions that invite students to investigate, to venture a prediction, to come up with a sensible plan, to collect data and figure out how best to organize it so it reveals patterns. Once students have gathered evidence, questions in the third stage (Draw Conclusions) invite students to think about what claims can be justified by the evidence and to come up with a possible explanation for their results. Finally, in the last stage (Communicate), teachers invite students to share their work with others by asking to whom they wish to present their work, what they want to say, and how they should say it. Clear, focused questions keep students' eyes on the prize and at the same time convey the message that the goal is for students to take ownership of their learning.

Asking just the right question is a skill, not only in science but also in literacy, social studies, and mathematics. Teachers admit it is hard work to learn how to ask better questions but believe it is worth the effort. Better questions result in more focused science talks and discussions, more complete and coherent science notebook entries, and more confident and independent learners who understand the purpose for their work and know what steps to take.

▶ Crafting Productive Questions

Improving questions and making them more productive is an ongoing process. Productive questions, a term adopted from Elstgeest, stimulate productive activity on the part of all students, promoting their abilities to think and reason scientifically. A teacher planning productive questions for an investigation must first ask himself what productive activity will look like as students move through the inquiry process.

Matching a Question to the Content and Stage of Inquiry

The types of questions that I use are definitely different across or throughout an investigation. As the kids start working, my questions come from what they are doing and what they are working on or puzzling over. My questions are based on what I see them saying, or noticing, or doing. I'm trying to get them to think more closely or deeply about the work that they're doing instead of jumping in and saying, "No, that's not what we're trying to do. Do this." I use questions like "Oh, why is that happening? What do you think?" or "Mmm, that's interesting. Can you tell me about it?" When we start closing the exploration, then my questions become more [like] "What was your evidence for that?" or "Why do think that? Where is your proof?" And I wrap up with the question that we started the investigation with and bring it back: "OK, so now what do you think and why?"

—KIRSTEN SHROUT, TEACHER, PERSONAL INTERVIEW

Productive questions always address the science content that is the focus of the unit or lesson. So in crafting questions, an important place to start is by clarifying the science concept or content that is the focus of the inquiry. Productive questions also promote the particular kinds of thinking and reasoning required during each stage of inquiry. At each stage of the Inquiry Learning Cycle, teacher questions that guide discussions, investigations, or notebook entries are designed to move students toward an increasingly solid understanding of the targeted science concept or phenomenon at the same time that they guide the inquiry process.

Take the case of a fourth-grade science unit on insects. One of the science concepts addressed in the unit is the life cycle. Students observe two insects, a monarch butterfly and a mealworm beetle, as they change over time. The teacher's questions are directed toward the idea of life cycle and, at the same time, reflect the purpose of the inquiry stage.

In the first stage of the inquiry cycle, the teacher brings a monarch caterpillar into the discussion circle. He says, "Yesterday I found this insect in my backyard; what do you think I need to do to keep it alive and healthy?" He follows up with these questions to introduce the second stage: "If we observe the caterpillar every day, what are your ideas about the changes we'll see? What are some ways we might record any changes in our science notebooks?" Students observe the caterpillar change into a chrysalis and then into an adult butterfly. Throughout the observation process, the teacher asks, "What do you notice? What changes do you observe?" Finally, to help students draw conclusions that focus on life cycle, he asks, "What can you say about the life cycle of the monarch butterfly based on your observations?" Following this experience, the students observe a mealworm and compare what they have learned about the two insects.

The teacher asks different kinds of questions at different stages of the inquiry, always focused on the big idea or concept of life cycle. He considers what will constitute productive activity—what he wants students to do, think, and talk about—at each inquiry stage and derives productive questions from these goals.

For example, at the Engage stage of the Inquiry Learning Cycle, productive activity includes students becoming aware of the ideas they already hold on the topic, identifying relevant experiences they've had, and raising questions. This is the time to provoke student curiosity and interest. This is the time to present materials to explore or an intriguing puzzle to consider. To capture students' interest and provide a common experience for everyone in the class, the teacher brings a caterpillar to the discussion circle and asks a question. The purpose of his question is to probe students' experience with the stages in the butterfly life cycle, in particular the larval stage. The question will

- prompt them to bring their ideas and experience to the surface

- encourage them to observe, wonder, and raise questions

- build on the common experience—in this case, looking at a real caterpillar— before they investigate the life cycle

In this stage, the questions are designed to welcome a wide range of responses and to prompt children to share the questions they have and things they wonder about. Other stages require differently designed questions.

So far, two characteristics of productive questions have been addressed: they (1) focus on science content and (2) match the purpose of the stage of inquiry. The next step is to take a closer look at characteristics of questions intended to be inclusive (person centered and equitable) and those designed to probe students' ideas, thinking, and reasoning.

Person-Centered Questions: Inviting Each Person's Ideas

Yesterday I found this insect in my backyard; what do you think I need to do to keep it alive and healthy? This question, at the Engage stage, clearly invites a personal response rather than factual knowledge or right answers. Now contrast the following three questions from an investigation on melting:

- How long will it take the ice cube to melt?

- How long do you think it will take the ice cube to melt?

- How long do you think it will take the ice cube to melt? Be sure to tell us reasons for your ideas.

The first question implies the teacher hopes for a right answer. The second suggests the teacher is interested in the students' ideas about melting. The third variation of the question asks students to explore the basis for their ideas about melting—to reason—and encourages them to think scientifically about what they know, reflecting on which variables (room temperature, size and surface area of the ice cube, etc.) may be relevant to this situation.

Science educator and author Wynne Harlen calls questions planned to elicit students' ideas *person centered*: "Person-centered questions are phrased to ask directly for the children's ideas, with no implication that one idea is more 'correct' than others. Subject-centered questions, by contrast, ask about the content in a way that suggests that there is a right answer" (2005, 61).

Compare these two questions:

- *Person-Centered Question:* What do you think you will observe when you add another bulb to the circuit?

- *Subject-Centered Question:* What will happen to the brightness when you add another bulb to the circuit?

Person-centered questions are crafted so that they invite students to articulate their own ideas, to reveal their own reasoning, and to think through the steps they themselves might take as they investigate.

Equitable Questions: Referring to Common Experiences

To be inclusive or equitable, it is not enough to invite each person's ideas. Some students come to the classroom without some relevant or common experience with the science topic or phenomenon. They can be left out of a discussion when the rest of the class is in the know and they are not. Providing a common experience, such as a brief trip outdoors, or bringing materials to the circle, or first providing an interesting challenge for students to explore, ensures that all students will have experiences from which to build ideas. Compare these questions:

- *Equitable Question:* When we went outside this morning, what did you notice about the clouds in the sky?

- *Inequitable Question (in Some Circumstances):* When you are in an airplane, what do you notice about clouds?

Open Questions: Avoiding the Yes-or-No Trap

So far, productive questions have been defined as those that (1) match the purposes and science focus of each stage of inquiry, (2) are person centered, and (3) are equitable. To encourage the ideas and explanations of all students, productive questions are usually open, inviting responses from students' varied and multiple perspectives. By contrast, closed questions can be answered by yes or no, or are questions that have only one right answer.

- *Open Question:* What are some ways that flowing water changes the surface of the land?

- *Closed:* Does flowing water change the surface of the land?

- *Open Question:* What does our data tell us about the relationship between the size and strength of magnets?

- *Closed Question:* Are bigger magnets stronger?

Having crafted a question, it's a useful practice to ask, "Can this be answered with yes or no or by a simple word or sentence?" If yes, you can tweak the question to make it open.

There are certainly appropriate times for closed questions. *How many days did the monarch butterfly remain in its larval stage? What happened to the pitch when we tightened the string on the door fiddle? What units will we use to measure the height of the plant?* Questions such as these provide both teacher and students with useful information at various points throughout an investigation.

Many teachers say that when they analyze their questions captured during a video-taped class, they discover that they ask many more closed than open questions. Asking more open questions is an effective strategy for establishing a science classroom where students' ideas and thinking are valued and visible.

▶ Conclusion

This chapter began with the premise that questions are a teacher's stock-in-trade. They can be an effective tool for focusing and guiding students' science inquiry learning, and crafting just the right questions requires hard work and thoughtful planning. Experience has shown that better questions lead to more talking, thinking, and independent and successful student learning. To hone their skill in crafting productive questions, teachers should start by making the science concept that is the learning goal crystal clear, first to themselves and then to their students. Next, they should consider the purpose of the stage of inquiry and craft a question that matches the stage and includes the science content. To probe students' ideas, reasoning, and thinking, questions need to be person centered. And for questions to be equitable, all students need to have relevant experience to draw upon. To invite the perspectives of all students, questions should be worded so they are open.

In the best of circumstances, teachers will do this work supported by resources and in collaboration with colleagues. With experience, teachers learn which concepts are likely to be most challenging and plan their questions accordingly. Like other skills, the facile use of productive questions comes from practice, feedback, revision, and reflection.

I couldn't develop a question alone. I think it's really so important to work with other people. I had a really great science coordinator. We would meet with each other once a week and I would tell her what we'd been doing. We wanted twenty or twenty-five minutes of good discussion. She would come in and observe the children and I would tell her about all the investigations. Then we would brainstorm. We would go back and forth. "OK, maybe we can ask this question. What would happen if we asked this question? What could they possibly say? This one is likely to end in five minutes, so forget about this question."

—GIZELLE DIZON, TEACHER, PERSONAL INTERVIEW

▌ For Further Reading

Cotton, Kathleen. 1988. "Classroom Questioning: Close-Up No. 5." *NWREL School Improvement Research Series* (May). Retrieved from www.nwrel.org/scpd/sirs/3/cu5.html.

This article provides a review of the research on classroom questioning and offers guidelines based on the research. Research findings are concerned with the relationship between teachers' questioning practice and student outcomes and are presented in several categories, including placement and timing of questions; cognitive level of questions; wait time; redirection, probing, and reinforcement; student attitudes; and teacher training.

Harlen, Wynne. 2001. *Primary Science: Taking the Plunge.* 2d ed. Portsmouth, NH: Heinemann.

This book makes the case for inquiry-based science and explains and describes a range of implementation strategies. It addresses directly how literacy is central to inquiry-based science teaching. The chapters "The Right Question at the Right Time" and "Helping Children to Communicate" pay particular attention to the connection between science and literacy.

CHAPTER 4

Science Inquiry and English Language Learners

Hands-on inquiry based science instruction provides opportunities for all students to develop scientific understanding and engage in inquiry practices. This type of instruction is especially promising for English language learners. Hands-on activities are less dependent on formal mastery of the language of instruction and thus reduce the linguistic burden on English language learners. Additionally small collaborative group work provides structured opportunities for developing English proficiency in the context of authentic communication about science knowledge.

—OKHEE LEE, "INTEGRATING CONTENT AREAS WITH ENGLISH LANGUAGE DEVELOPMENT FOR ENGLISH-LANGUAGE LEARNERS"

In many classrooms across many U.S. states and districts, a substantial number of students do not speak English as their first language, and the English language abilities of students in a given classroom may span a broad range. When connecting science and literacy, it is therefore critical to consider approaches for supporting English language learners. This chapter highlights some assumptions about how inquiry-based science supports the learning of both science and language of English language learners and draws attention to a few specific strategies and cautions.

▶ Assumptions

Five basic assumptions, based on current research about teaching inquiry-based science to English language learners, are important for teachers to bear in mind when there are ELLs in their classrooms.

1. Inquiry-based science teaching, with direct experience and collaborative work at its core, is particularly accessible to ELLs because the engagement is through direct experience, not language alone, and learners can demonstrate their understanding in multiple ways (e.g., drawing, demonstrating with materials).

2. Inquiry-based science teaching is a meaningful context in which ELLs can develop language skills, particularly if teachers provide some adaptations and additional support.

3. All students bring an array of experiences, theories about the world, and cultural understanding to their science learning in school. These diverse backgrounds contribute to their own learning and enrich the learning of others.

4. While it is important for teachers to be aware of differences in the linguistic backgrounds of the students in their classes, it may be even more important for teachers to understand diversity in the cultural practices relating to language. Examples of cultural practices to consider are the role and structure of argumentation and presentation; group discussion norms and expectations; and the use of narrative, fantasy, and humor. With awareness of their students' cultural practices, teachers can implement teaching strategies based on this understanding.

5. Many strategies, emphases, structures, and scaffolds that are helpful to ELLs are beneficial to native English speakers as well.

▶ Strategies

By its nature, inquiry science includes a culture of respect and openness in which students who do not speak English as a first language can thrive and provides opportunities for them to practice language skills by talking and listening in group discussions. English language learners also benefit from the direct experience with the natural world; opportunities to elicit prior knowledge, which encourage students to make connections to what they already know; the collaborative work, which requires discussion of a common experience; and the use of varied forms of representation in science notebooks and class charts, which provides choices other than text.

In addition, teachers with English language learners in their classrooms should also consider the following instructional strategies, all of which are likely to benefit many other students in the classroom as well as those learning English.

- *Reduce the language load* by using real objects as focal points for discussion; using and having students use visual organizers to illustrate key points; illustrating concepts through demonstrations or role-playing; and monitoring instructional language for difficult vocabulary, lengthy sentences, or complex structures.

- *Support whole-group discussions* by providing opportunities for small groups of students to discuss their observations and questions before the whole group convenes, using turn and talk, allowing wait time, speaking slowly and clearly, honoring students' use of words in their own language, and recognizing and valuing their growing use of English. Explicitly teach and model these discussion skills for the benefit of everyone in the class.

- *Teach vocabulary* by focusing on a small set of key terms, introducing new words and ideas in the context of students' investigations, and displaying new words alongside a picture or artifact in a readily visible place. This strategy contrasts with expecting students to learn science vocabulary before they have had any experience with actual objects or phenomena with which to associate names or terms.

- *Use students' first language* where appropriate and possible.

- *Encourage pictorial and graphical* as well as textual representations of ideas and information.

- *Provide scaffolding* for writing, such as sentence stems, frames, graphic organizers, and key vocabulary so that students can convey their thoughts without struggling with format.

- *Connect the work to familiar experiences* by making explicit links to students' experience and cultures and inviting students to share their cultural experiences.

- *Establish groups for inquiry work* that place students who are learning English with students who are effective at encouraging participation of everyone in a group.

- *Use multiple assessment strategies,* with an emphasis on performance assessments and interviews, so that students understand the question and can demonstrate their knowledge and understanding of science in different ways.

▶ Cautions

In teaching English language learners, teachers can experience some common pitfalls, which may be problematic for native English speakers as well. They include the following:

- focusing solely on the decoding, definition, and meaning of new words so that the science class becomes a phonics lesson, a vocabulary lesson, or a language arts lesson

- attributing student silence to a lack of ability or understanding, as opposed to a language difficulty

- confusing a lack of language and writing proficiency with a lack of knowledge

- using only assessment strategies that rely on language rather than including performance assessments where actions can demonstrate knowledge and understanding

- focusing on vocabulary and technical aspects of writing, such as conventions and grammar, rather than thinking, reasoning, and ideas

▶ Conclusion

Inquiry-based science with strong connections to literacy incorporates a number of elements that support the science and language learning of English language learners. To be successful, however, teachers must be aware of the language needs of their students and emphasize instructional approaches and strategies such as those recommended here. In doing so, they will increase the learning opportunities for ELLs and, at the same time, meet the needs of all their students.

▶ For Further Reading

Amaral, Olga Maia, Leslie Garrison, and Michael Klentschy. 2002. "Helping English Learners Increase Achievement Through Inquiry-Based Science Instruction." *Bilingual Research Journal* 26 (2): 213–39.

This article reports on a study of the impact of a kit-based science program on English learners. Researchers measured student achievement in science, reading, writing, and math for students participating in the Valle Imperial Project in Science (VIPS) program. Findings showed that student scores were higher in all four disciplines relative to the amount of time (between zero and four years) they were in the program.

Ballenger, Cynthia. 1997. "Social Identities, Moral Narratives, Scientific Argumentation: Science Talk in a Bilingual Classroom." *Language and Education* 11 (1): 1–14.

This article describes how students in a bilingual classroom were able to effectively engage in science talk even though they were initially not familiar with standard discourse in school science. By allowing students to enter the conversation through different avenues, such as jokes and personal stories, and bring more of themselves to the dialogue, the teacher helped these students become engaged in the discussion without having to relinquish their personal intentions. As the discussions progressed, students were jointly developing new ways of arguing, evaluating evidence, and theorizing.

Hill, Jane D., and Kathleen M. Flynn. 2006. *Classroom Instruction That Works with English Language Learners*. Alexandria, VA: Association for Supervision and Curriculum Development.

This book is an application of the earlier work *Classroom Instruction That Works* (2001) by R. Marzano, D. Pickering, and J. Pollard using an ELL lens. The practical strategies discussed are intended to support teachers as they help all elementary students, at all levels of English language acquisition, succeed.

Lee, Okhee, and Mary A. Avalos. 2002. "Promoting Science Instruction and Assessment for English Language Learners." *Electronic Journal of Science Education* 7 (2).

This article discusses science teaching and assessment as it relates specifically to English language learners. The authors describe how the importance of science for ELL students is not just in the learning of science, but in literacy development, English language proficiency, mathematics, communication, and habits of mind. The paper also discusses the current status of science instruction and assessment for ELL students, as well as policies and practices that have proven successful for ELLs.

Lincoln, Felicia, and Caroline Beller. 2004. "English Language Learners in the Science Classroom." *Science Scope* 28 (1): 28–31.

This article offers strategies for use by teachers of English language learners in order to meet the needs of ELL students without diluting the content. They include the following: set goals before adapting the curriculum; list and repeat lesson objectives and instructions; use simple language, not simple concepts; demonstrate science concepts; increase wait time; encourage student collaborations; and include language-minority parents. A checklist for cultural and language differentiation is also included.

Rosebery, Ann S., and Beth Warren, eds. 2008. *Teaching Science to English Language Learners: Building on Students' Strengths*. Arlington: NSTA Press.

This book is a collection of chapters and teacher reflections about issues pertaining to improving science instruction for English language learners. Chapters tackle topics such as teaching from students' strengths and teaching academic language. The chapters are intended to be of use for teachers and many are written as classroom case studies. The book includes a number of teacher reflections.

SECTION TWO

The Role of Talk in Science Inquiry

Children need time to talk, verbally or in writing, yet when time gets short, talk is what is pushed out of the curriculum first. But, for many of us, it is talk that leads to understanding and helps us process what we are learning.

—PATRICIA BLOEM, "CORRESPONDENCE JOURNALS"

The important role that talk plays in learning in all subjects is more and more acknowledged. Balanced-literacy programs have carefully guided discussions about books and writing. Many new research-based mathematics curricula include math talk as a critical part of instruction. Because of the importance of such discussions to science learning and to the development of an understanding of the nature of science as a collaborative endeavor, this book places a strong emphasis on the role of discourse, or talk, in science. The "Further Reading" section at the end of each of the two chapters in this section includes resources that review the research into the role of talk in science and literacy learning and describe practical applications of the research in the classroom.

Talk is important not only for science learning. Social constructivist theories based on the work of Lev Vygotsky (1934) are widely accepted in education and suggest that talking with peers and teachers promotes students' cognitive development in ways independent work cannot. Lauren Resnick expands on these basic ideas, suggesting that

> *not all talk sustains learning or creates intelligence. For classroom talk to promote learning, it must have certain characteristics that make it accountable. Accountable talk seriously responds to and further develops what others in the group have said. It puts forth and demands knowledge that is accurate and relevant to the issue under discussion. Accountable talk uses evidence in ways appropriate to the discipline (for example, proofs in mathematics, data from investigations in science, textual details in literature, documentary sources in history). Finally, it follows established norms of good reasoning. Accountable talk sharpens students' thinking by reinforcing their ability to use knowledge appropriately. As such, it helps develop the skills and the habits of mind that constitute intelligence-in-practice. (1999, 44)*

The two chapters in this section focus on whole-group discussions because they are hard to carry out in the classroom and also because they are particularly important in science, where it is critical to share multiple perspectives, weigh different claims, and debate ideas. The first chapter, "A Culture of Talk," addresses how to create the necessary classroom norms and expectations for respectful student-to-student discussion. Chapter 6, "Classroom Talk," focuses on discussions that happen at two important parts of the Inquiry Learning Cycle.

Whole-group discussions can take place at many times and for many purposes during an investigation. Both the purpose and the stage of the Inquiry Learning Cycle influence the nature of the discussion and the facilitation strategies used by the teacher. Chapter 6 examines discussions that take place at the beginning of a unit of study or a new investigation and those that take place at the end of a unit or investigation, when there is data to discuss and there are conclusions to be drawn. Whole-group discussions also are important when students plan how to conduct an investigation—what procedures to use and what data to seek in response to the question at hand. But since the student skills and facilitation strategies needed are similar to those of making-meaning discussions, the chapter does not address planning discussions.

In the following quote, Kirsten Shrout, a third-grade teacher, suggests the powerful connections between science and literacy discussions as well as some of the differences.

> In read-aloud and in reading workshop, I do a lot of teaching up front in the year about basic things like sitting, how you look at someone when you're talking to them, and body language. Then we move into "OK, this is how when someone says something we agree with, we can acknowledge that." . . . And then also how to disagree. For third graders and young children, disagreeing is very hard. I teach them that it's OK to disagree but you need to do it in a respectful way. . . .
>
> That work really lends itself naturally to the science work. In reading, it's not as tangible. There's a book, and we have ideas, and we grow ideas as readers, but with the science work there's a lot more tangible evidence for them. I think they had an easier time having conversations and agreeing and disagreeing or questioning what someone said because they had their notes right there. They remembered doing the work. In reading, we talk about how readers can have all sorts of ideas. We all have different reading experiences because of our background, knowledge, or our personal experiences. It's harder for them to navigate those conversations. In the science work we were doing, that conversation seemed a lot more natural for them. I hear them say, "Oh, Jack, I completely agree with you because here in my notebook . . . ," or "When I was doing this, this is what happened and that sounds exactly like what you were doing," or "Wait a second, Natalie. I'm not sure I get what you're saying or that I agree with you because I found something different. This is what happened when I did . . ." They had that personal experience in the investigations to back up their talk.
>
> —KIRSTEN SHROUT, TEACHER, PERSONAL INTERVIEW

CHAPTER 5 | **A Culture of Talk**

Teacher: If we want to look for worms for our investigation, where do you think we should look?

Briana: I'd look under a flat rock because I've found a couple of worms there sometimes.

Malakai: You could probably find some in a pile of dirt.

George: A garden because there's lots of soil and lots of things for worms to eat.

Kali: I'd say a garden, too, because I know worms help things grow by letting water into the soil.

Samantha: If you see stuff growing in the garden, you know worms are in there.

Jose: We were digging in our mulch pile, and we saw lots of worms but not all in the same place. There weren't many on top. Most were at the bottom because it was dark and damp and cool.

Briana: That's what it's like under the flat rock I was talking about—dark and damp and cool.

Kali: But what about a garden that's got the sun shining on it, making it hot?

Jose: Maybe when the soil gets hot or dry, the worms go down like they did in our mulch pile.

George: So even if there are things for worms to eat, if it's too hot and dry, maybe worms go somewhere else.

The Importance of Talk

As they launch their study of earthworms with a discussion of good places to look for worms, these fourth graders recognize that they already have relevant ideas and experience about earthworms and their classmates do, too. As they talk to one another, students' ideas and questions begin to grow.

Talk is an important part of doing science. Scientists share data, discuss their results, debate their conclusions, and present findings. For students of science, just as for scientists, talking about their experiences and the data they have collected helps them make connections, clarify their thoughts, generate conclusions, develop theories, and ask new questions. In other words, talking with peers and teachers promotes students' cognitive development in ways independent work cannot.

When students (or nonstudents) talk about ideas and thinking with others, they rehearse, rethink, and revise their ideas. When students are given a chance to talk about what they are thinking and learning throughout a science investigation, they are likely to consider what they already know, examine prior experiences, try to make sense of data, defend their reasoning, and entertain new ideas and perspectives. Hearing peer comments allows students to compare their ideas with those of others, challenge what others are saying, and modify their own ideas as needed.

Opportunities to talk occur in all areas of the curriculum and serve similar purposes. For example, in literacy, students learn to talk and develop their ideas about text. During interactive read-alouds, teachers pose questions about a text and facilitate discussions that help students reflect on what they think about the text and explain the basis of their ideas. Students also talk when they work in pairs in reading partnerships. Here, the teacher models and guides students as they practice talking with a partner, asking one another questions, and disagreeing respectfully. In many classrooms, small groups come together in what are called *literature circles* to share, discuss, and debate interpretations of a book they have read, citing specific words or passages to support their ideas and explain their thinking. If teachers make it clear to students that they are using similar skills and strategies when they discuss their work in science and if they highlight the differences, students can often apply the discussion skills they have learned in literacy to science.

Building students' capacity for engaging in quality science talk supports both students' science learning and their oral and written language development. But despite the knowledge of the importance of talk, it is not given a high priority in most schools and, thus, is often neglected in the classroom. Reasons for this vary, but competition for time is often one of them. Another is teachers' inexperience with facilitating discussions where students move beyond sharing experiences and results to probing one another's ideas and using evidence to argue and debate ideas and explanations. Teachers also may be uncomfortable with the unpredictability that goes hand in hand with an invitation to discuss ideas. But because of the importance of talk, the message is clear: not only is talk permitted in classroom learning; it is required.

Small- and Whole-Group Discussions

In science inquiry classrooms, students have many opportunities to engage in discussions as they work together in small groups. These important discussions tend to happen naturally when interest is high and the purpose is clear. As teachers move among groups, they should encourage this talk, help students learn and use norms of good talk, and guide it to be more purposeful when necessary. This opportunity to share and debate thinking in smaller groups can serve as a rehearsal time for students, helping them prepare to participate in whole-class discussions or to write their ideas in science notebooks. Small-group discussions are more fruitful when students understand the purpose and are accountable for results. For example, the fourth graders quoted at the start of this chapter, who were investigating worms, had been given time in their small groups to discuss their ideas before coming to a whole-group discussion. Later they met in their groups again to design their earthworm investigations. They knew that each group would be accountable for a drawing on chart paper that showed the design the group had agreed upon.

> *I've videotaped in the classroom for them to see how they're talking. I did it a lot with the small groups at first. I would play it back to them and ask, "OK, what did you notice that was happening over here?"*
>
> *And they would say, "Malik was talking the whole entire time."*
>
> *I'd respond, "Well, how does that feel? What about the other three students that are not talking?"*
>
> *And Malik would actually say, "Yeah, I'll let Jennifer talk more next time." That was a really important huge breakthrough for them to actually see themselves on videotape.*
>
> —GIZELLE DIZON, TEACHER, PERSONAL INTERVIEW

Unfortunately, effective whole-group discussions or science talks are far less common. Typically, what is called *discussion* is actually a series of teacher-student-teacher interactions in which students try to answer the teacher's questions rather than struggle with their own ideas and the ideas of the group. At other times, a whole-group discussion may consist of a prolonged exchange between one student and the teacher. The teacher may probe that student's ideas but not open the discussion to the rest of the group. In some cases, the class is gathered to listen to every student describe his data without an opportunity to make meaning of the class' collective findings.

There are many reasons for the lack of effective discussions. To become proficient at sharing ideas, debating, supporting ideas with evidence, and clarifying what another person has said, students must receive explicit instruction. To be successful, both small- and whole-group discussions also require an environment or culture with a set of norms and expectations in which students are comfortable sharing thinking, challenging one another, and taking risks. Putting all this in place takes time and explicit instruction.

The rest of this chapter focuses on developing students' abilities to participate in successful whole-group discussions and to learn valuable skills, norms, and expectations.

▶ Characteristics of Whole-Group Science Discussions

If you were to drop in on a science discussion in a classroom with a culture that supports serious science talk, you would likely notice most or all of the following characteristics (Douglas et al. 2006, 47–48):

- The students are seated in a circle facing one another.

- There is a set of explicit norms and expectations, posted in view of all.

- There is a natural flow to the conversation with a good deal of student-to-student interaction rather than a question-and-response exchange with the teacher.

- Many students participate: the conversation is not dominated by a single student or by the teacher.

- The conversation is focused: students linger on a particular idea and make connections to one another's ideas.

In this classroom, it is likely that everyone assumes that ideas and experiences are shared and that all thoughtful and interesting ideas are valued. Following is a closer look at some of these characteristics.

The Circle

The arrangement of the physical space can affect the quality of discussions. When students are in a circle—in chairs, at desks, or on the floor—everyone can see and hear everyone else without turning her body. Students cannot have their backs to the speaker or hide behind another student or engage in side conversations. Listening is made easier, and the expectation that everyone is part of the discussion becomes implicit. The circle also fosters an intimacy and accountability to the group that cannot be achieved when students are spread throughout a classroom. When teachers join students in the circle, it also becomes easier for them to facilitate rather than dominate the discussion.

> *The circle is important because the students can face each other. They can see each other. And when one person is sharing, everyone is able to zoom into that person and hear what that person has to say.*
>
> —SHARON SEALY, TEACHER, PERSONAL INTERVIEW

Norms and Expectations

Whole-group discussions by people of any age group require an explicit set of norms and expectations that are accepted by everyone. Some classrooms may have already established norms and expectations for whole-group discussions that take place during literacy, social studies, or mathematics. These norms likely have been generated with student input, taught, and practiced. In this case, applying them to science discussions often happens naturally. Where this is not the case, the class must spend time developing a list of discussion norms, learning how to follow them, and practicing them in many contexts. A basic list might include openness to new ideas, respect for others, participation by everyone, and mutual accountability. And students might need to learn certain skills such as taking turns, listening to others, responding to one another, staying on focus, and disagreeing respectfully. These norms and expectations create the foundation for the other characteristics of effective whole-group discussions.

> *Children obviously need to be taught how to have a discussion. And the pieces I think that they need to know and that make for a really great full-class discussion are active listening: being able to listen to each other and being able to respond to what somebody else is saying. The thing that we work the most on is not to be caught up in what you want to say but to be a listener and then to be able to respond to another kid—to really have a conversation.*
>
> —AMY FLAX, TEACHER, PERSONAL INTERVIEW

> *Listening was a challenge and we worked on it. If someone is going to speak, we have to respect and listen to each other, not just . . . be quiet. There's a difference in being quiet and listening to what the other person is saying.*
>
> —SHARON SEALY, TEACHER, PERSONAL INTERVIEW

Student-to-Student Interaction

A number of teaching strategies focus specifically on increasing student-to-student interaction. Perhaps the most important and most difficult for many teachers is simply to be quiet and let students talk. The habits of asking questions one after the other, keeping the pace up, and repeating what students have said are hard to break. But if the teacher continues to dominate the airtime and the substance of a discussion, student-to-student discussion is unlikely. Another habit that many students and teachers find difficult to break is raising hands. Over time and with practice, students can learn to enter a discussion and to let others enter without the adult or a chosen student deciding who speaks next. This is very important for effective discussions, because when teachers call on students, they often interrupt the flow of the conversation, thus taking away any responsibility from the students for managing the discussion.

One strategy for creating a more natural flow in class discussions is to generate a list of what students do when they talk with their friends over lunch. When students talk informally, they use a variety of discussion moves beyond simply agreeing or disagreeing. They add to what someone else has said, ask for clarification, wonder about an idea, suggest a new idea, challenge, debate, analyze, question, or tell a story to make a connection. Making connections to their informal discussion skills can help students participate effectively in formal classroom discussions. It is also helpful to develop a list of phrases students can use to push the thinking of a peer: "Why do you think that?" "Can you say more about that idea?" "I was wondering about . . ." Additionally, it is often necessary to teach and practice specific skills including taking turns, keeping eyes on the speaker, and listening respectfully. Teachers can use short mini-lessons to model these specific skills.

Full Participation

Getting all or as many students as possible to participate in the discussion is critical. Students, however, are less schooled in this notion than in how to listen to teachers and provide the right answer when asked. Less confident students and English language learners often are reluctant to participate. Perhaps the most important strategy to encourage participation by more students is wait time. Both research and experience testify to the power of waiting five or even ten seconds after asking a question or asking for comments before letting students respond. During this time, students are instructed not to speak or raise their hands. Instead, they sit and think quietly. The time helps students formulate and clarify ideas and prepare to participate in the discussion. It helps not only the students who contribute less frequently but also those who respond immediately but often without having thought very deeply.

Another strategy is to have students turn and talk to a partner. This allows students to try out what they want to say and build confidence in their ideas. Many reluctant talkers can be encouraged to participate in the whole-group discussion if they first turn and talk. A teacher might also give students time to prepare for a discussion by asking them to review their science notebooks, do a quick-write, or talk briefly in their work groups, so that they are more likely to come to the whole-group discussion with something to say.

Staying on Focus

Keeping the discussion focused and on topic can be difficult for students, especially if they have experienced many discussions in which people shared their ideas one after another rather than built on the ideas of others. Modeling appropriate interactions and redirecting the conversation can help students become responsible for staying on topic on their own. Teachers might model how to respond to someone's ideas using phrases such as "Could you clarify what you mean?" "That's interesting, but my data shows . . . ," and "I agree with that because . . ." They may encourage someone to question what has been said: "Matt, I think you had a different idea than Maria. Can you share that with her?" And they may intervene if the students go off on a tangent: "That's a really interesting comment, but we need to focus back on . . ." or "Keep that thought and we will come back to it if we have time. Right now we are . . ."

Science discussions lean on students' experience, evidence, and observations, and these provide the content that fuels lively science talks. Sometimes, if a discussion of a particular idea is flagging, giving students a two-minute break to refer back to their notebooks or to turn and talk may generate more conversation about the idea or question. As students talk with a partner, teachers can listen in. When the break is over, they can share a couple of the ideas they heard, synthesize some of the thinking that was generated, or ask a pair of students to share their thinking.

▶ Conclusion

Effective whole-group discussions do not just happen. They require a classroom culture in which students respect and trust one another and are comfortable sharing thinking, challenging one another, and taking risks. Ideally, such a culture exists throughout a school or is a shared goal of a group of teachers. In any case, to create such a culture, teachers must model respect and openness to the ideas of their students. Effective whole-group discussions also require teaching students the range of necessary skills. The next chapter, "Classroom Talk," examines gathering-ideas and making-meaning discussions along with the student skills and teacher-facilitation strategies they require.

▶ For Further Reading

Chambers, Aidan. 1996. *Tell Me: Children, Reading, and Talk*. Portland, ME: Stenhouse.

> This book offers guidelines and suggestions for how to support students as they learn to talk about their thinking. It describes how providing a forum for sharing thinking enables students to grapple with ideas and come to some collective understanding, which in turn leads to deeper understanding.

Chapin, Suzanne, Catherine O'Connor, and Nancy Canavan Anderson. 2003. "The Tools of Classroom Talk." In *Classroom Discussions: Using Math Talk to Help Students Learn, Grades 1–6*, 11–42. Sausalito, CA: Math Solutions.

> The authors of this chapter discuss five "talk moves"—actions that teachers can take to promote constructive conversations and support mathematical thinking: revoicing, prompting students for further participation, asking students to restate someone else's reasoning, asking students to apply their own reasoning to someone else's reasoning, and using wait time. They also discuss three "talk formats"—whole-class discussion, small-group discussion, and partner talk—along with rules for talk. The authors provide four case studies to illustrate these moves and formats and to demonstrate how a culture of talk is created in the classroom.

Gambrell, Linda B., and Janice F. Almasi. 1996. *Lively Discussions: Fostering Engaged Reading*. Newark, DE: International Reading Association.

> *Lively Discussions* emphasizes why classroom discussion is important and offers specific strategies for how teachers can help students build discussion skills. Although the book focuses on reading, these are clearly skills that students can use to deepen their science learning as well. The book includes examples of children participating in discussion activities that emphasize interacting with peers and constructing meaning.

Kuhn, Leema, and Brian Reiser. 2006. Structuring Activities to Foster Argumentative Discourse. Paper presented at the annual meeting of the American Educational Research Association, 7–11 April, San Francisco.

The focus of this paper is on scientific argumentation and how classroom practices can inhibit or foster student contributions. The authors discuss the epistemological and social challenges of argumentation in the classroom and offer three design strategies that incorporate both of these elements in order to foster scientific argumentation: create a need for students to use evidence, create a need for students to argue, and make the epistemic criteria explicit. The authors then illustrate the application of these design strategies by describing their pilot study in a seventh-grade classroom.

CHAPTER 6 | Classroom Talk: Gathering-Ideas and Making-Meaning Discussions

The talk during and after each experiment with the circuits also looked much like the book talks we had during reading workshop. While they were working in small groups, students would exclaim at what they were observing and then share with one another, asking questions, disagreeing, and checking results by testing again together. Everyone eagerly participated in the small-group conversations. Our whole-class conversations had some quiet listeners, but toward the end of the unit, as more and more students felt comfortable with the content and with the ideas they were growing about electricity, the more they participated in our big discussions. They would debate ideas, question one another, and even look back into their notebooks to offer proof for their ideas.

—KIRSTEN SHROUT, THIRD-GRADE TEACHER, PERSONAL INTERVIEW

In Chapter 5, the case is made that not only is science talk permitted in classroom learning, but it is required. The rationale for this strong statement is twofold. Scientists depend on discussion and debate with peers as they refine their procedures, evaluate data, test the strength of their conclusions, and present their findings to others for review. To understand how scientific knowledge is generated, students benefit from similar conversations with peers about their investigations. In addition, talking promotes cognitive development when students clarify their ideas or check their reasoning as they talk it through with others.

In the same chapter, characteristics of purposeful classroom science talk are identified, as are some strategies and skills for fostering such whole-group discussions. Whole-group discussions are particularly important at certain stages of the Inquiry Learning Cycle (see Chapter 1): when students begin an inquiry or investigation; when they design an investigation and collect the data they will need to answer their questions; and when they are coming to conclusions about their work. These discussions share many basic features, but because the purposes for each are somewhat different, some of the skills the students need and some of the facilitation strategies teachers use also vary. This chapter focuses on the discussion at the beginning of an inquiry or investigation (a gathering-ideas discussion) and the discussion at the end (a making-meaning discussion).

▶ Gathering-Ideas Discussions

Gathering-ideas discussions take place when students begin to explore a new idea or question at the start of a new unit. This kind of discussion may also happen before a new investigation within a unit or even partway through an investigation if a new idea surfaces. It is closely tied to the Engage stage of the Inquiry Learning Cycle. The teacher introduces the topic by providing an opportunity for students to make connections to their prior experience or knowledge. He might set the stage with a question or a demonstration or let students explore the target phenomenon through open exploration with materials.

For example, in the opening of Chapter 5, "A Culture of Talk," a group of fourth graders discuss good places to look for earthworms. On the surface, the teacher's discussion question, *If we want to look for worms for our investigation, where do you think we should look?* might seem to ask for practical advice; in fact, a response requires students to consider their relevant prior knowledge and experience with earthworms. The discussion reveals that these students are not starting their study of earthworms from scratch.

In another example, third-grade students prepare for a gathering-ideas discussion at the start of a study of sound by having a brief open exploration of the way sound changes when a guitar string is tightened, loosened, shortened, or lengthened. Then, when these students talk about their ideas about sound in the discussion circle, everyone is able to draw on this exploration to formulate ideas, questions, and wonderings about sound.

Gathering-ideas discussions are designed to activate students' prior knowledge and experience; generate ideas, questions, and wonderings; and spark their interest in pursuing those questions. The teacher's role is to encourage all students to share their own ideas and experiences but also to broaden their experience through listening to others. The teacher encourages students to interact, but the focus is on raising questions, clarifying, or adding on to what someone has said rather than on debating or arguing. A gathering-ideas discussion also provides opportunities to write. Students may jot down ideas to prepare for the discussion or they may add a written response to the discussion question in their science notebooks after the discussion wraps up. Using discussion to activate prior knowledge is very similar to what students do when they are introduced to a new text in a balanced-literacy program.

Having a gathering-ideas discussion is not the same as creating a K/W/L (**K**now, **W**ant to Know, and **L**earned) chart. Although K/W/L charts are used in many classrooms, they are often unfocused and elicit wide-ranging free-association responses, allowing students to stray far from the focus of the upcoming investigation. For example, if students are beginning to study the properties of water drops, there is a difference between the prior knowledge that will be activated in response to *What do you* *know and want to know about water?* and *What are some of the things you have noticed about water when you take a bath or fill a glass with water?* The latter question is more specific to the investigation and focuses on properties of water.

Also, a gathering-ideas discussion is not a direct assessment or quiz of what students know about a topic. Nevertheless, it is likely to reveal some of what they know, how they are thinking, and some of the naïve conceptions they hold. For example, a discussion of water may reveal confusion about where water goes when it "disappears."

The Role of the Teacher

Beginning the Discussion

The role of the teacher in a gathering-ideas discussion is first and foremost to identify a productive question. For example, when beginning a study of water drops, a question such as *What do drops do on a plastic plate?* is not very useful for a gathering-ideas discussion because students have not yet had an opportunity to investigate, and many are unlikely to have specific knowledge about the behavior of drops. The more open-ended question *What do you think you will see when you put drops of water on the plate?* allows students to draw from their prior experience and share tentative ideas. Finding the balance between a question that is too open-ended and one that is too specific is part of the crafting of effective questions. Preparing for a good discussion also requires that teachers consider students' prior experience. If students have little experience with a phenomenon, it is helpful to let them explore with materials first. For example, in a unit on simple machines, students might explore a variety of tools before coming to a gathering-ideas discussion. If students are already familiar with the phenomenon, open-ended exploration may not be necessary; however, physical objects and materials can still help focus the discussion. For example, if students are going to investigate evaporation, the teacher might place a wet dish rag on a plate in the center of the circle and ask, "What do you think will happen if we leave this dish rag on the plate overnight? Think first and in a moment we'll discuss your ideas."

For some students, taking a few minutes to do a quick-write in their science notebooks prior to the discussion, as they do in balanced literacy, allows them to collect and generate their thoughts in preparation for the discussion. Books also can serve as a stimulus for engaging students in a gathering-ideas discussion; however, it is best to select books that are more descriptive or evocative rather than just informational; informational books give students "the answers" and reduce the likelihood that they will share their own emerging ideas.

Facilitating the Discussion

During a gathering-ideas discussion, the teacher reinforces classroom norms and expectations, encourages all students to participate, and supports student-to-student talk. He guides the content by redirecting the discussion if it strays too far from the topic and probing, where appropriate, for more details or for reasons why something has been said. He asks clarifying questions, pushes gently for students to say more, and invites students to explain the experiences that have contributed to their thinking. As he does this, he models and encourages the interactive strategies he wants his students to use with one another. At the close of the discussion, the teacher summarizes briefly the range of ideas that have been shared without trying to synthesize, evaluate ideas, or come to any group conclusions.

Perhaps most importantly, teachers must resist the temptation to engage in direct instruction; this is hard to do. Students may well have naïve, erroneous, or incomplete ideas, but direct instruction at this stage would interfere with the learning goals of the discussion and reduce the powerful learning that will take place later in the investigation as students explore the phenomenon, collect data, and come to conclusions.

The teacher may choose to record students' initial ideas and check back on students' understanding at the end of the unit. But in this kind of discussion, the purpose is not to arrive at a conclusion or consensus nor to provide answers to questions. Rather, it is an opportunity for students to make connections with what they know and to hear the ideas of others. For the teacher, it is an opportunity to gauge the level of understanding of his students and adjust his instruction accordingly.

> I let them know in many cases there's not a wrong or a right answer. It's what you're thinking. I also remind them that we can help each other. When one person gives an idea, it makes the other person think about it and we can all get a lot of ideas. And it's OK to have the same idea after someone says it. Letting them know that it's OK to say whatever is on their minds took away that fear of not being right.
> —SHARON SEALY, TEACHER, PERSONAL INTERVIEW

▶ Making-Meaning Discussions

Making-meaning discussions take place when students have completed an investigation, a series of investigations, or a full inquiry unit and there are conclusions to be drawn. They are closely tied to the Drawing Conclusions stage of the Inquiry Learning Cycle.

The purposes of making-meaning discussions are to interpret findings and raise new questions about what has been learned. Making-meaning discussions also provide an opportunity for students to attempt to explain a phenomenon and hear the explanations of others. During a making-meaning discussion, students focus on the data in their science notebooks and the data collected by the whole class. They look for patterns or relationships in the data and for claims that can be made from the evidence. During these discussions, students may have to deal with contradictory evidence or new questions. Debate and argument about ideas and claims lead to a conclusion, to a new question, or to a determination that more data is needed.

When we were doing the work with conductors and nonconductors, they had a lot of different answers that sometimes conflicted. One person would say, "Oh, a paper clip conducts electricity." And another kid would say, "No, it doesn't." And they were OK saying, "Oh, that's interesting; let's go back and keep testing it." Instead of me saying, "OK, paper clips do conduct electricity," they [had] the experience of finding that answer. It makes the experience more authentic and more fun instead of just a teacher saying, "Hey, this is what happens," or "This is the answer." They get to discover it for themselves.

—KRISTEN SHROUT, TEACHER, PERSONAL INTERVIEW

Having a making-meaning discussion is not the same as sharing results. In a simple sharing, students, one by one or group by group, report what they have done and what happened. One student's or group's report is rarely connected to the reports of others. In discussions of this type, there is little need for students to listen to one another nor is there opportunity for discussion, debate, or comparison of claims, evidence, and explanations.

A making-meaning discussion is also not a time for the teacher to quiz students about their knowledge. This would focus student attention on the teacher and on giving the right answer rather than promote discussion and debate.

The Role of the Teacher

Beginning the Discussion

Just as in gathering-ideas discussions, a clearly stated question is key to a good making-meaning discussion. Usually, this is the question that defined the investigation. To illustrate, imagine a study of changes of state—in this case, evaporation. The students have placed containers of water in different parts of the classroom with thermometers nearby and have documented the gradual disappearance of the water. After collecting data over several days, they see that the rate of evaporation varies in different places. They come together for a making-meaning discussion in response to the question *What do you think is the relationship between evaporation and temperature?* They then put differently shaped containers in the same place and again observe and record their data. This is followed by another making-meaning discussion focused this time on the question *What difference do you think the shape of the container makes in the rate of evaporation?* With several investigations and making-meaning discussions under their belts, the students end their study of evaporation with a making-meaning discussion of the original investigation question: *What factors do you think influence the rate of evaporation of water?*

Making-meaning discussions are based on work done and a rigorous examination of data to identify data that can support a claim. Once selected, the supporting data is referred to as evidence. Because of the challenging nature of this work, it can be helpful for the teacher to give students the opportunity to prepare for the discussion. She may ask them to discuss their findings in small groups first and come to the full group with notebooks in hand. Another strategy is for students to create a simple poster that includes their investigation setup (if different from other setups), claims, and evidence. It also is important for students to have shared the procedures used and data collected prior to the discussion. Depending on the topic, this can be done by compiling individual data in class charts; having groups make data charts and post them; or encouraging small groups to meet with one another to share findings.

Facilitating the Discussion

The teacher plays a more active role in facilitating making-meaning discussions than in gathering-ideas discussions. As well as reinforcing the norms and expectations, she must work hard to keep the focus on the investigation question, push for analysis and debate, and guide the discussion toward either a conclusion all concur with or toward a new set of questions and investigations.

Making-meaning discussions challenge students and require new skills and strategies. Students must learn to build on the ideas of others and also to disagree respectfully. They need to state their claims, back them with evidence from their notebooks, and defend their reasoning. They also need to listen to the ideas of others and modify their own ideas if appropriate. The teacher's role is to model and support these skills and this reasoning and, at the same time, release responsibility to the students as much as possible.

Bringing Closure

At the close of the discussion, the teacher provides a clear synthesis statement of what the discussion has achieved. This may be a group conclusion or a decision to collect more data. This is also the time to clarify any confusion about what has been agreed upon and to correct any misinformation. In some cases, the conclusions students reach may be inaccurate not because of faulty reasoning or misinformation on the part of the students, but rather from insufficient experience or data. If the teacher chooses to provide a more scientifically accurate conclusion, she needs to do so carefully; simply telling students that their conclusions are wrong may undermine their confidence in their abilities to investigate and reason from evidence. Statements such as the following are useful: "That claim is certainly supported by the evidence you have. Typically, scientists would want more data before considering evidence . . ." or "Scientists who had time for more extensive investigation found that . . ." or "That's a very thoughtful claim you are making. I think we need to go back and try . . . and see if it holds up."

> *I'm OK with kids coming up with different answers that might not be the right answer or the answer that's in the book because I know that they're still growing*

ideas and their thinking. As they keep working and I'm questioning them or they're questioning themselves and they're gathering evidence and doing observations, their thinking will continue to change. And I think the important part is getting them to see that it's OK for your thinking to change, that you don't have to get an answer and stick to it.

—KIRSTEN SHROUT, TEACHER, PERSONAL INTERVIEW

It is critical to make time for this wrap-up; as time runs out in the science period, it is often omitted. Closure at the end of a discussion allows everyone to hear what has been said, what has been learned, and what the next steps will be. Making time for closure also conveys the message that the thinking and work students have done are valuable and worthwhile.

Recording Classroom Discussions

It is important to have a permanent record of the results of class discussions, including ideas that have been shared, conclusions and explanations that groups have arrived at, and new words that have emerged in the discussion. This is particularly useful for visual learners and English language learners.

Teachers make these records in a variety of ways. Often, teachers jot down ideas on a chart as students raise them. One drawback of this charting is that the discussion often slows as teachers write. A second drawback is that what goes on the chart may not be what is most important to retain. An alternative strategy is for teachers to take notes as the students are talking. After the discussion, drawing from the notes, teachers can summarize the group's thinking and write the summary on a chart they post. Alternatively, they can seek the students' help in identifying the important ideas that were raised and chart those. In both cases, the end result is a synthesis or summary of the *thinking*, not a record of all that was said.

Conclusion

Whole-group discussions take time and effort. Teachers must instruct students in discussion norms, expectations, and speaking and listening skills. They must provide time for students to practice and must help students make connections to the skills they have learned during literacy instruction. But just as they do in literacy instruction, large-group discussions play a specific role in science learning. They are as critical to the development of understanding in science as are the direct experiences. They provide opportunities for students to listen to the ideas of their peers, defend their own ideas, ask more refined or focused questions, develop deeper conceptual understanding, and become more fully aware of the collaborative nature of science.

▶ For Further Reading

Dawes, Lyn. 2004. "Talk and Learning in Classroom Science." *International Journal of Science Education* 26 (6): 677–96.

The focus of this article is on strategies used to foster talk between students in the science classroom. The authors first discuss children's ideas about science, teacher interventions, issues surrounding group work, and how to promote an environment where group talk can support science learning. They then report on the Thinking Together project, which considered whether teaching children ways to talk and think together could raise their science and math achievement. Both observational and test data showed that student engagement in exploratory talk did lead to higher achievement in science.

Maloney, Jane, and Shirley Simon. 2006. "Mapping Children's Discussions of Evidence in Science to Assess Collaboration and Argumentation." *International Journal of Science Education* 28 (15): 1817–41.

The purpose of this study was to look at the decision-making skills that children use in science and whether or not they use evidence. Students participated in collaborative activities and discussions that were further analyzed by the authors, who established four "levels" that related to an argument's sophistication and students' use of evidence in making arguments. The authors reason that children can learn to argue effectively if given the opportunity to participate in similar collaborative activities that include discussions of evidence.

Newton, Douglas P. 2002. *Talking Sense in Science: Helping Children Understand Through Talk.* London: RoutledgeFalmer.

Talking Sense in Science suggests that while hands-on investigation and recording are present in some elementary science instruction, the role of talk as a tool for sense making is often overlooked. This book aims to help teachers use talk to guide children to deeper science understanding.

Norton-Meier, Lori, Brian Hand, Lynn Hockenberry, and Kim Wise. 2008. *Questions, Claims and Evidence.* Portsmouth, NH: Heinemann.

The authors' premise is that traditional science writing in school, the lab report, only involves students in a process scientists use when reporting their work to a wider audience. Scientists also use a particular style of argumentation (including questions, claims, and evidence), which is missing from most classrooms and essential for students' science learning. This is a practical approach to helping teachers include more scientific argumentation in their science program.

Varelas, Maria, Christine C. Pappas, Justine M. Kane, Amy Arsenault, et al. 2008. "Urban Primary-Grade Children Think and Talk Science: Curricular and Instructional Practices That Nurture Participation and Argumentation." *Science Education* 92 (1): 65–95.

This study looked at how children worked together to sort "ambiguous" objects into solids, liquids, and gases and to explain their decisions. The children were purposely not told what part of the objects to focus on, and they identified four different ways to classify the substances: macroscopic properties, prototypes, everyday functions, and process of elimination. The authors discuss how children's understandings were influenced by their social roles, and they note the value of teaching practices and activities that do not lead children to a single answer, opening ideas up to debate and further promoting engagement with the science.

SECTION THREE

Writing in Science

Writing is a tool of science. It is through writing that scientists make and keep a permanent record of their work, and writing is an important way through which they communicate with their peers and the public. As they practice science, students and scientists keep science notebooks containing their questions, procedures, data, and thoughts, written over the duration of an investigation. They also produce polished pieces for a wider audience based on the work they have done and recorded in their notebooks. But writing in science is not only for communicating with others; it also is a tool for learning that supports scientists and students alike in clarifying thinking, synthesizing ideas, and coming to conclusions. This book discusses writing and talk in separate sections, however, in the classroom they are inextricably linked. Small- and whole-group discussions are often rehearsals for writing conclusions and reports, and quick-writes before a discussion can start ideas flowing. Discussion pushes students to clarify their ideas before they write their conclusions or write a more formal piece about their science experiences.

Students need many of the basic writing skills they learn in literacy if they are to make effective use of writing in science. The two chapters in this section focus on the science notebook and writing about science investigations for an audience. They describe the clear links between instruction in science and writing as well as some of the differences teachers and students need to be aware of. The links between science and writing instruction are mutually reinforcing. When, in the authentic context of science, students apply and practice the writing skills they have learned, they become more fluent and flexible in the use of those skills. And when they use writing in science, they deepen their understanding of both content and the practice of science.

Keeping science notebooks provides the opportunity for students to use many literacy strategies to organize their data, evidence, and thinking, including bulleted lists, charts, labeled drawings, and diagrams as well as brief notes and observations. When writing more formally about the science they have done, students draw on what they have learned about writing to a variety of audiences in a variety of ways. They may write a report, a narrative, a persuasive chapter, or a how-to book. They also may choose to write poetry, realistic fiction, or a story. Whatever genre they choose, their writing draws from their notebooks and reflects a synthesis of understanding of the concepts and the process of their science inquiry. It demonstrates both science knowledge and knowledge of appropriate conventions of print, literacy skills, and use of science vocabulary. When science writing begins with students' own work, they both hone their literacy skills and deepen and apply their science understanding.

Each of the two chapters in this section highlights the important links between writing and science and the win-win advantage of writing in science. Each also points to important differences that can be useful to students in understanding the literacy conventions and language of science as distinguished from those of the language arts. However, an important take-home message is that the excitement and interest that inquiry-based science generates in the classroom creates an ideal context for writing for students, especially those for whom writing is difficult.

CHAPTER 7 | **The Science Notebook**

Putting entries into the notebook as an inquiry progresses is an important aid for organizing thoughts, interpreting results, or preparing the ground for further inquiry. For many scientists, the notebook must be on the bench, open and ready, before work can begin. When it has been filled with history, it is a very important silent partner in an ongoing research effort.

—JEROME PINE, "THE SCIENCE NOTEBOOK" (UNPUBLISHED PAPER)

The science notebook is an indispensable tool for doing science in the laboratory and in the field. When students are engaged in a science inquiry, they are recording the story of their inquiry—what they did, what happened, the data they collected, and what they thought—just as a scientist would. Their notebook entries must be clear, complete, and concise so that others can challenge the data and replicate the procedure. This chapter describes the purposes of the science notebook, how it is developed, and how it is used. It emphasizes the intimate connection among thinking, talking, and writing: talking helps students clarify their thoughts before they write in their notebooks, and writing helps clarify thinking and oral communication. At the end of the chapter are three notebook samples from three different classrooms, which are accompanied by brief comments.

Purposes of the Science Notebook

The science notebook is the ongoing record of the thinking and process of a scientific inquiry. It is used in a variety of ways depending on the stage and nature of the inquiry. As students explore a phenomenon during the Engage stage, they might make lists of words that describe the phenomenon or an object, make drawings, or record what they think they know and what they would like to find out about the phenomenon. They may speculate about how an object might change over time or react to an event. As an investigation unfolds during the Design and Conduct Investigations stage, students use their notebooks to write their questions and their predictions, present their procedures, record their data, and document their growing understanding, as well as record new questions that arise. As they enter the Draw Conclusions stage, notebook entries become sources of data for analysis, as well as records of claims, evidence, and possible explanations. Finally, the notebook as a whole provides students with a record of their work that they can use to inform more formal presentations, reports, and other writings that communicate to a broader public.

> *Students have to have a place to record what they're doing in science; otherwise, it would just be playing with materials. The notebook gives them an opportunity to see what they're doing daily and how that changes.*
> —SUZANNE NORTON, TEACHER, PERSONAL INTERVIEW

The science notebook, however, is more than just a record of a science inquiry; it is an indispensable tool for supporting students' reasoning and deepening their conceptual understanding. When students formulate and clarify a question and make a prediction as they begin an investigation, they are encouraged to use their knowledge and prior experiences. As they determine what data to collect and how to collect it, students must think about their question and predictions, the nature of the evidence they will need, and how to record that evidence so that it will be useful to them later in the investigation. Writing reflections, including speculations and initial ideas, pushes students to think about their questions in relationship to growing amounts of data. Making a claim requires carefully analyzing data and connecting evidence to the claim. It means refining ideas and initial theories. Proposing explanations pushes students to bring their ideas together, infer cause and effect, and refine or create new theories.

A science notebook is not a collection of stuff. In many classrooms where hands-on science takes place, students keep their written work in some form of folder or science journal. Typically, however, these are different from the science notebooks described here. Science folders or journals may be collections of worksheets or periodic entries, but they are not organized, daily, authentic records of investigations similar to what a scientist would keep.

A science notebook is also not a personal diary. Calling it a science notebook, not a journal, emphasizes this distinction, because the word *journal* often connotes a more personal, informal type of writing. In many classrooms, students keep journals, using them to express feelings, relate experiences, or retell stories. A science notebook may have wonderings, speculations, and comments, but the focus is on questions, predictions, procedures, data, analysis, and emerging theories based on firsthand experiences.

> *The more we've used the notebooks and had the science talks, the better kids are getting at understanding the science. It's forcing them to be responsible for what they learn in science and giving them the opportunities to ask more questions, look back at what they did, and recognize how they've learned. How could you go back to something that you didn't record anywhere? So it's critical that there's a place where we go back . . . to look at our thinking about how it's changed. We don't get that opportunity a lot.*
> —SUZANNE NORTON, TEACHER, PERSONAL INTERVIEW

A science notebook is not a place for practicing writing, although students will use many writing skills in this very authentic context. While emphasis on correct spelling, grammar, and complete sentences is appropriate as students learn to write, when they craft notebook entries, priority should be given to expressing thinking and observations clearly and efficiently; in other words, if a word can be clearly understood, correct spelling can take a backseat for now. In science, students also learn that graphs, drawings, and bulleted lists are effective ways to record data and are often preferable to complete sentences.

Finally, the science notebook is not the same as a writer's or reader's notebook. In literacy instruction, students use reader's notebooks to record their ideas and thoughts, wonderings, reactions, and snippets of dialogue. They use their writer's notebooks to experiment with different genres of writing. The contents are for their personal use and may have minimal structure. The purpose of science notebooks differs. Although the science notebook is also a place for reflections, wonderings, and questions as the inquiry progresses, there is a structure imposed by the science inquiry process itself that determines much of what the students include. A science notebook is not only for a student's personal use; in science, a record of an inquiry must be open for others to read, discuss, debate, and use to replicate procedures.

> *In the past, I think we were teaching science and using notebooks and notebooks were beautiful. I mean, kids' drawings of science, their plants growing, the little charts— they always look[ed] very appealing. But I'm not sure how much the kids were learning other than just recording things. The notebooks were just a place to draw what we had done maybe each day. Now, when I look at the notebooks after all these conversations that the kids have, I'm beginning to see that they aren't just recordings of daily experiences. Kids are able to write what they understand. And I'm not sure that I saw that before.*
>
> —SUZANNE NORTON, TEACHER, PERSONAL INTERVIEW

The science notebook samples at the end of the chapter provide examples of the work of three students—Destiny, Emilia, and Erin—in three different classrooms. These are not exemplary. They each have strengths and areas of weakness and show the work of students (and their teachers) learning to use the science notebook as an integral part of learning science.

▶ Skills for Using Notebooks

Students need to learn many literacy and science skills and develop certain habits if science notebooks are to become an integral learning tool in science. To successfully make entries of all kinds in their science notebooks, students need to develop their scientific vocabulary as well as a number of specific expository writing skills.

Some basic writing skills are likely taught during literacy instruction but need to be reinforced and modeled as students learn to use them to write and record in science. These include strategies for organizing writing, procedural writing skills, and making bulleted lists. Other skills needed for science notebooks, such as the use of charts and graphs, may be taught in mathematics.

One of the ways that I've encouraged the authentic use of science notebooks is by telling them stories. My sister is a scientist and I tell them stories about how my sister does experiments. I've shown them examples of the notebooks and what they look like. They would notice the charts and that it was dated. I wanted them to see models so that they could know what their notebooks should look like.

—GIZELLE DIZON, TEACHER, PERSONAL INTERVIEW

Some of the thinking and reasoning skills students learn and use in science as they do their investigations and write in their notebooks are similar to the skills they use during literacy, and making that connection is important. But there are other skills that are called by the same name when, in fact, they are different. Here, clarification is needed so that students learn to use these important skills appropriately for each setting. One example is predicting. When students predict in reading, the prediction is based on their interpretation of the author's intention. In science, a prediction is based on the student's prior experience and knowledge of a natural phenomenon. Inferring is another example. In literacy, inferences are based on a combination of what is in the text and the reader's prior experience. In science, inferences are based on observations and data. A third example is making detailed observations. In science, these must be as objective and specific as possible and often include diagrams and labeled drawings, whereas in literacy, observations in words and images may be more subjective. If students are accustomed to keeping a writer's or reader's notebook, instruction should highlight the differences.

Elements of a Science Notebook

Although a notebook entry or series of entries may have a number of possible structures and formats, the notebook includes all of the following elements:

- *Basic Information:* This includes the date and, if appropriate, time, temperature, and other details.

- *A Statement of Purpose:* This is a clear, concise statement or question that defines the purpose of the immediate investigation in relation to the larger purpose of the unit. To the extent possible, students should generate and write these statements, but if the teacher generates a question for the whole class, it can be printed and stapled into the notebook. Emilia's notebook on magnets includes an example of a lengthy but clear statement of purpose.

- *A Prediction:* Not all investigation questions invite a prediction. Where a prediction is appropriate, it always should be accompanied by a reason or an explanation ("I think so because . . ."). Both Destiny's notebook about germination and Erin's on erosion include predictions, although not consistently throughout.

- *A Plan or Procedure:* To be complete, notebooks should contain the procedure for each investigation. If students generate the procedure, they should write it in their notebooks themselves. If the teacher provides the procedure, it can be printed and inserted into the notebooks so that students do not have to spend time copying.

- *Data:* Data must be recorded in the science notebook in a clear, efficient, and organized way. Students can record data in many ways, including making drawings, charts, or graphs or writing text. Students should help design and select recording strategies. If the recording format is a chart, graph, or Venn diagram, however, it may be more efficient to provide students with the format rather than have them draw it. As their graphic literacy develops, students learn that the same data set can be displayed in more than one way and that some displays are more effective than others for conveying patterns or observations. The three notebook samples provide examples of a range of strategies for displaying data, including Destiny's clear and detailed drawings, Erin's charts and bulleted lists, and Emilia's graphs.

- *Regular Reflections:* At the end of most entries, students should write a brief statement or two describing their current thinking as well as questions that may have come up ("Today I am thinking that . . ."; "It looks like . . ."; "I'm wondering about . . ."). A good example of this is in Emilia's science notebook entry "Testing Magnets," dated 11/20.

- *Periodic Conclusions:* At appropriate moments during a unit, when students have finished an investigation and are moving on to another part of the same unit, they should write a somewhat more formal notebook entry about learning and thinking at that point in the study. At this point, students look at the investigation question, make a claim, and provide supporting evidence ("Based on what I did, I think . . ."; "I think that . . . and the evidence is that . . ."). This is followed by a brief tentative explanation ("I think this may be so because . . ."). Again, it is Emilia's work that provides a good example, in her entry "What I Can Say About Magnetic Strength," dated 11/30/06.

- *Final Conclusions:* At the end of a unit of study, the notebook contains a final conclusion. In this synthesis of the entire study, students move from their specific claims to a more general conclusion about the overall purpose or question of the unit ("After looking at my notebook, I think that . . ."). The conclusion clearly states what was found out and relates this explicitly to the evidence from the work. It includes explanation and reflection and, if appropriate, new questions and next steps. This conclusion becomes the starting point for communicating with others through a more formal report or other forms of writing.

Each entry in a notebook will include only those elements relevant to the particular stage of the investigation or unit. If the science class period consists of a discussion of the events of a previous day, the notebook entry may simply include a reflection on the discussion. If the science class time is used to continue an experiment, the entry will simply pick up from where the experiment left off at the end of the previous class.

Facilitating Notebook Use

The development of skills and abilities for notebook writing takes time; students can take responsibility for different elements of notebook entries only as they develop the needed skills. Teachers must explicitly teach and model what is important to include in an entry, the nature of the thinking and reasoning, as well as ways to write notebook entries.

The ideal notebook starts as a set of blank pages (lined, unlined, or graph paper), as in Emilia's case, which gives students the freedom to structure and organize their entries. In this ideal notebook, students are fully responsible for all parts of the notebook, creating a record of their experiences and thinking. But to get to this point, students must go through many steps, learning the necessary skills, slowly assuming responsibility for the notebook, and, perhaps most importantly, making the science notebook an essential part of doing science. Figure 2 suggests a trajectory for turning over to students the responsibility for notebook elements.

As students start to use science notebooks, the most important elements to turn over to them are those that require them to draw upon their own experiences and thinking: writing initial ideas and reflections. Right from the start, they learn that their thinking is important and that communicating it in writing can be both challenging and helpful in clarifying what they think and why. The next step is to help students master those elements that require more sophisticated scientific reasoning: forming predictions and drawing conclusions. These require more teacher support but are still very much based on students' own thinking and the thinking of the group. Students need to develop not only the skills but also the confidence in their ability to use them.

While Figure 2 provides a suggested sequence for releasing responsibility to students, there is no clear trajectory for all students or groups nor do all students move toward independence at the same rate. Regardless of sequence, the writing and scientific reasoning skills required for science notebooks have to be modeled and explicitly taught, either during literacy time or in science class. Spending time talking about each element, modeling possible approaches, and sharing and critiquing one another's work can help students improve their thinking and their notebook entries.

Most students will benefit from some scaffolding as they learn to organize and keep their notebooks, such as a notebook page with a prompt ("My prediction is . . . because . . ." or "I think that . . . My evidence is . . ."). Of the three notebook samples, both Destiny's and Erin's show simple scaffolding that their teachers have provided to support their data collection. Others will benefit from class charts of suggested starting points and examples of different data-collection structures to choose from. Under

Teacher-guided inquiry   Student-developed open inquiry

$\longleftrightarrow$

Elements	Early Stages	Middle Stages	Later Stages	Student-Led Inquiry
Initial ideas, experiences, wonderings	S	S	S	S
Question	T	T	T/S	S
Prediction	T/S	S	S	S
Procedures	T	T	T/S	S
Data recording	T	T	T/S	S
Data analysis	T/S	T/S	S	S
Reflection	S	S	S	S
Conclusion	T/S	T/S	S	S

T: Teacher responsible for element
T/S: Teacher and student share responsibility for element
S: Student responsible for element

FIGURE 2 Student and Teacher Responsibility for Notebook Entries

most circumstances, copying is not helpful. It does not deepen students' scientific reasoning skills or understanding and uses valuable time. A procedure, question, or conclusion that is to be used by the whole class should be printed, handed out, and stapled or glued into the notebook.

▶ Authentic Use of Notebooks

Scientists keep notebooks *on* their work because they need them *for* their work. The notebook contains the data for their analyses. If they get contradictory results from an experiment, they go back to see how they did their earlier investigations. If a peer questions their data, they go back and check or redo an experiment. If they have to write a report for a funder or an article for a journal, they rely upon this record of their thinking and experimentation.

For students to understand the role of notebooks in science and take advantage of the potential of the science notebook for developing understanding, they must use notebooks constantly. Every science lesson should begin with taking out their science notebooks. Students also must use them authentically in the classroom and not just to meet the expectations of the teacher. To encourage this authentic use, teachers might ask students to

- review what they did the day or week before as an introduction to the day's work

- review their notebook and choose one idea or question to talk about with a partner

- organize their data to share with the class

- review their thinking of a week ago and how it has changed

- check back on a procedure to see why their results differ from the results of another group

- write a synthesis, conclusion, or report

In these ways teachers can help students see the value not only of the notebook as a whole but also of its various elements and characteristics.

> There are lessons I did with notebooks that had to do with rereading entries and jotting down in the margin, or on a new page, or at the bottom of the page, things like "Oh, I did used to think this, but now I'm thinking this because . . ." We did a lot of that work both in readers' and writers' workshop, where they would go back and reread and reflect on different entries and ideas that they'd written about previously. That definitely came into play in their science notebooks. I would just say, "OK, before we start our work today as scientists, let's reread our notes from yesterday," or "Before we start talking, let's reread our notes." And they had their notebooks and their pencils, so after a conversation they could write such things as "Now my thinking has changed because Jack said blah, blah, blah. Now I need to go back and try this out or test this again because he's got me questioning what I did."
>
> —KIRSTEN SHROUT, TEACHER, PERSONAL INTERVIEW

▶ Teachers' Use of Notebooks

Science notebooks benefit the teacher as well as the learners. Notebook entries are a rich source of formative assessment data that can be used to craft constructive feedback for students. Helpful feedback refers to a specific notebook entry, describes its strengths, and raises questions that will prompt the student to reflect upon the entry. Such feedback enables the student to know what steps to take to make the entry more effective. Formative assessment also provides teachers with information that can guide their instruction. A quick review of notebooks may reveal the need to revisit an idea, provide a mini-lesson on graphing, or repeat a procedure. The commentary accompanying each of the three sample notebooks provides brief examples of data that might be collected by a teacher to guide her next instructional steps.

Learning from students' notebooks and providing feedback to students requires that teachers read notebook entries on a regular basis. After a decade of study of students' learning through the use of science notebooks, Fulwiler (2007) found that teachers can provide the most effective feedback if they assess the notebooks three to five times during a six- to twelve-week unit, in addition to checking to be sure students are writing in their notebooks during the course of a lesson. Fulwiler also recommends assessing notebook entries after a series of lessons that target the development of a specific concept or skill. These periodic assessments include providing written feedback on individual students' notebook entries.

A final note: While some teachers use science notebooks for assigning grades, caution should be used. The notebook is only one part of the work students do in an inquiry-based science class and only one of the ways that they can demonstrate their skills and understanding. Furthermore, a significant body of research supports the view that student learning is maximized when feedback on notebooks is nonjudgmental and does not include grades or rubrics (Harlen 2005; Black and Wiliam 1998; Fulwiler 2007).

Conclusion

Notebooks are a critical tool in scientific inquiry. They can take many forms depending on the subject matter and the particular need or preference of the scientist or, in this case, of the teacher and her students. Regardless of form, however, all science notebooks share these common characteristics:

- They are chronological, written records of an investigation: the doing and the thinking.

- They are clear, detailed, organized, and structured.

- They are used at all stages of the Inquiry Learning Cycle to document, reflect on, and review work in progress.

Effectively using science notebooks requires many different skills. Students learn some of these skills in literacy instruction and mathematics and apply them as they use their science notebooks. Some skills are similar to those in other domains but must be understood in the context of science. Others are specific to science and must be taught at that time. Effective use of notebooks also requires that teachers provide regular feedback to students about their notebooks and provide opportunities for their authentic use.

▶ Notebook Samples

Following are three examples of student notebooks. They have been chosen to illustrate a range of topics, structures, grade levels, and work that is typical for these age levels. The commentary on each identifies strengths and areas for growth from three perspectives: the organization of the work, the effectiveness of the communication, and evidence of student reasoning. Included as well are examples of instruction that might move the student's work forward.

Notebook Sample 1: Destiny Investigates Plant Growth (Grade 3)

Teacher: Sharon Sealy

These notebook entries were made in May as Destiny and her classmates investigated the growth of beans. Previously, the class had planted a bean seed in soil and observed it growing, flowering, and producing a new seed. In this investigation, students focused on the changes occurring during the germination process that they couldn't observe when the seed was underneath soil. Their question was *What happens when a bean seed starts to grow?*

The students had been keeping science notebooks all year, and for this investigation, Sharon prepared sheets with two side-by-side observation strips that could be taped together to make a foldout record showing changes over time. With this accordion foldout design, students could look back and more easily compare changes from day to day and predict what would happen next. Sharon also provided sticky notes if more space was needed, and Destiny used them to extend her thoughts.

Destiny's drawings show great detail and accuracy. The observation sequence is chronological, clear, and easy to follow. At various times, Destiny has included a prediction, questions, and some of her reflections to supplement the drawings. The final piece of writing, "How to Plant a Bean," is somewhere between a conclusion (claim, evidence, and explanation) and a piece of more formal writing about the whole experience. It reflects her understanding of the needs of plants (water, space, air) and the growth sequence (germination, leaves, flowers, and then seeds), although not all key stages are mentioned (e.g., there is no mention that the root appears first, then the stem, then the leaves).

Reading this notebook, a teacher will notice weaknesses in Destiny's use of conventions of print, but as this is a science notebook and her meaning is clear, these weaknesses should be addressed as part of literacy instruction, not science instruction. Destiny's drawings are quite remarkable, demonstrating how closely she has observed, but she needs to work on extending her descriptive language. Sharon might work with her directly, or if this is also a challenge for other students, as is likely, she might highlight descriptive language in the science discussions. The structure of the notebook supports the effective organization of the data; however, Destiny needs to make sure that she includes the investigation question and predictions regularly. A list of notebook elements for the whole class might be effective. Finally, Destiny needs guidance in developing a conclusion and presenting it briefly in her notebook.

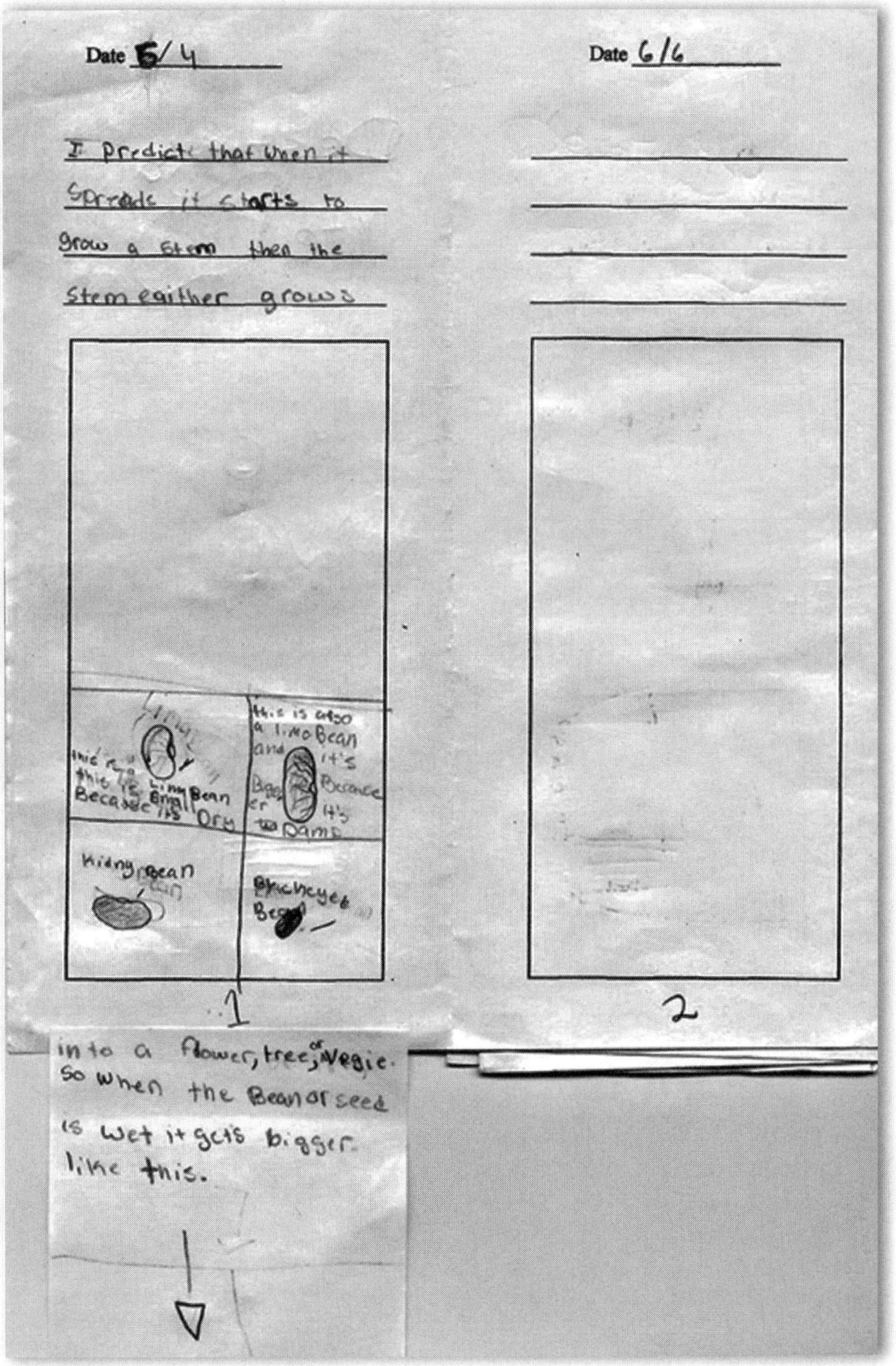

Date 6/4

I predict that when it
Sprreads it starts to
grow a Stem then the
Stem eaither grows

Date 6/6

This is also
a lima Bean
and it's
Bigg Because
er it's
so Damp

This is a
lima Bean
Inside
this is Small
Because its Dry

Kidny Bean

Blackeyeb Bean

1

2

into a flower, tree, or vegie.
So when the Bean or seed
is wet it gets bigger.
like this.

DESTINY'S NOTEBOOK page 1

Date 6/6

I just observed
that the kidny
Bean just sprouted
why is the plant going
inside the paper?

Kidny Bean
is
sprouted

it just
sprouted

Fact
When I first looked at
it I was observing
I also measured it and
it's 3½
cm

3

Date 6/7

Today my prediction
came true because
I predicted that
The plant will be

it's also becoming

Kidny
Bean

4

longer and it
came true it has
some roots coom-
ing out of the
plant. Fact

Yesterday it was
3½ cm now it's
6 cm

DESTINY'S NOTEBOOK page 2

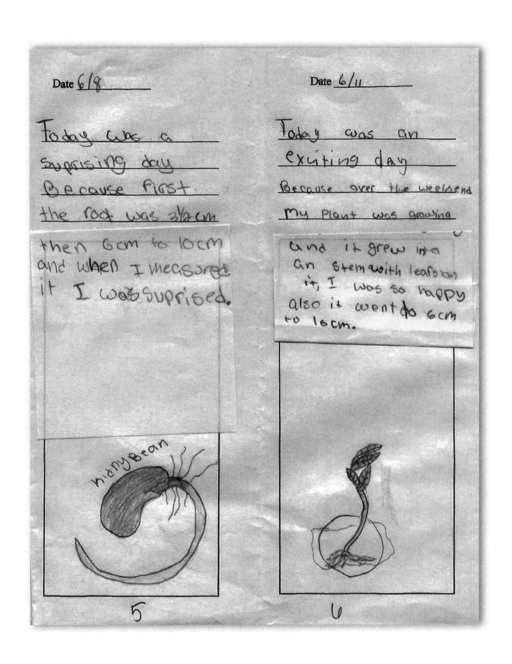

Date 6/8

Today was a
suprising day
Because first
the root was 3½cm
then 6cm to 10cm
and when I measured
it I was suprised.

himyBean

5

Date 6/11

Today was an
exciting day
Because over the weekend
my Plant was growing
and it grew into
an stem with leafs on
it, I was so happy
also it went to 6cm
to 16cm.

6

DESTINY'S NOTEBOOK page 3

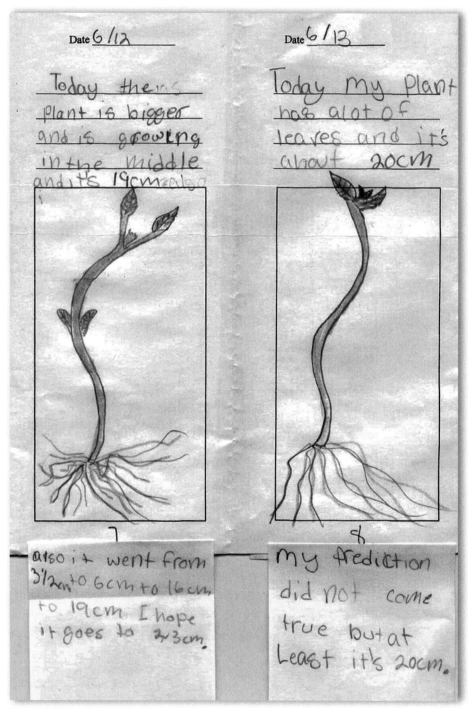

Date 6/12

Today the ms
plant is bigger
and is growing
in the middle
and it's 19cm also

7

also it went from
3½cm to 6cm to 16cm
to 19cm. I hope
it goes to 2,3cm.

Date 6/13

Today my plant
has a lot of
leaves and it's
about 20cm

8

My prediction
did not come
true but at
Least it's 20cm.

DESTINY'S NOTEBOOK page 4

How to plant a bean

How to plant a bean is that first you get a pot then yo put dirt then put the bean and you water it and allways let it have room and air so it can get realy big you can write about what you observe about it and then when your done you can put your plant outside and put it in the ground. When your plant is bigger that means that you are doing a good job. When your doing a good job that means your following the steps like watering it, giving it room, and give it air. When you put it out side it's going to grow more leaves and Beans But first its going to have flowers then beans.

By: Destiny

Notebook Sample 2: Emilia Investigates the Strength of Magnets (Grade 5)

Teacher: Suzanne Norton

These notebook entries were made in November as Emilia and her classmates were investigating the strength of magnets and the question *What factors affect the strength of magnets?* They started by using a procedure specified by a published curriculum. When they looked at their data, the students found it inconsistent and felt their procedure produced results that could not be replicated and was, therefore, unreliable. They decided to come up with a new procedure. This notebook sample picks up where Emilia wrote her conclusion concerning the procedure and suggested another procedure. The magnets the students used for the basic investigation were rubber-coated square stackable magnets. The notebook then provides a record of the new procedure.

The class had used this type of plain science notebook in an earlier investigation, and students were encouraged to record not only procedures and data but also their thinking, reasoning, and questions as they occurred throughout an investigation.

Emilia's notebook entries demonstrate very strong communication and organizational skills. She uses labeled drawings to show her procedures and results and shows with a graph how adding magnets to the stack affects strength. Her thinking and reasoning are expressed clearly and in detail. The conclusion includes the investigation question, a claim (stackable magnets are much weaker than bar or cow magnets), evidence (reference to her tests), and possible explanations (the rubber won't let out all the magnetic strength or the size matters).

These notebook entries show that Emilia is beginning to understand how to use graphs to display her data. Suzanne needs to work with her (and others who might be at the same level) to check her graphs and any accompanying explication to see that they include all the necessary information. For example, the graphs of how the number of magnets changes in force over distance need titles and some further explanation about the two factors she is considering (number of magnets and whether they were lying flat on the table or standing up). Emilia's thinking is clear from this work and there are clear directions Suzanne could take to extend the investigation and deepen Emilia's understanding. For example, Suzanne might encourage her to pursue the surprising results with bar magnets or think more deeply about whether the new procedure was indeed better.

Magnet Strength   11·16·08

After conducting 2 experiments to test the strength of our magnets, I think that it is unfair to judge there strengths. I think that because the washers that we were testing with, were different sizes. So if some people had more of the thicker washers, then the magnets would have held less. And if some people had more of the thinner washers, the magnet would have held more. That is why I think that so many people had different conclusions. That is why I conclude that it is unfair to test the Magnet stregths with the washers.

I think that the first 2 experiment to test the strength of our magnets was not the best way to tes magnet strengths. I think that because the tounge depreser could have decreaces the amount of washers that the magnet could have held. A better way (in my opinion) for testing the strength of our magnets would be to

put a magnet on a desk or a table, and get an
object that is attracted to a magnet. Then to see how
far you can put the object untill the magnet will
not attract the object any more. That, in my opinion
is a better way to test our Magnet Strengths.

Testing Magnets Strengths   11·20

Based on our Science Talk on Friday, we relized that the first way we tested the magnets was not the best way to the magnets. So we decided that we would test the magnets a different way. The way that we think is a better way to test the magnets is that we will put the magnets on a flat surface see how far the magnet starts to attract a paperclip We think that this is a better way to test the magnets because everybody (I am estimating) will get the same answer.

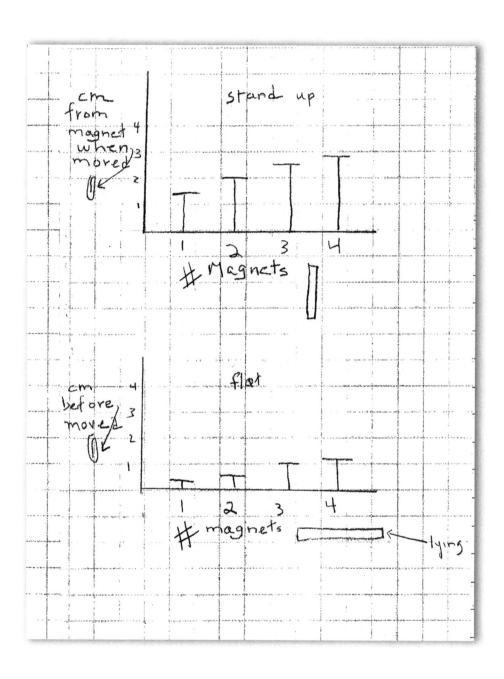

EMILIA'S NOTEBOOK page 4

Testing Magnets   11·20

One thing that supprized me in my results was
the magnets are stronger when they stand upright.
It supprized me because I would have suspected that
both sides would be equal. I would have thought that
the magnet would have the same strength everywh

Testing Magnets   11·27

Today, I tested with a bar magnet. One
thing that supprised me was that the sides of
the magnets are stronger than the ends. I
also found out that the South end of the
magnet was stronger than the North end.
These things supprised me because on
almost every side, there was a different
strength. I would have thought that at
least only 2 sides would have different
strengths.

What I Can Say About

Magnetic Strengts   11:30

What can I say about magnetic strength—

Now, after the tests that we have been doing. I can say that our magnets are much, much weaker ~~than~~ than bar or cowmagnets. One reason that I think that is because our magnets have rubber over there surface. I think that the rubber affects the strength of the magnet because it would not let all of the magnetic strength out. My evidence of this is that throughout many tests, the bar or cowmagnet is much stronger. But, one thing that makes me not so sure about this is that the bar and cow-magnets are quite a bit bigger. So that might mean that they are stronger anyway.

Notebook Sample 3: Erin Investigates Effects of Flowing Water on Soil (Grade 4)

Teacher: Amy Flax

These notebook entries were made in May as Erin and her classmates were investigating how various processes continually shape and change Earth's surface. In this teacher-developed unit, the students began with a focus on the role of water and the question *How does flowing water change the surface of the land?* The students used stream tables to observe patterns of rapid change as water flowed over different types of soil (clay, humus, sandy soil) and observed how the three soil types layered when they were vigorously mixed with water and then allowed to settle.

This was the class' first experience using notebooks rather than a worksheet packet. Each student received a bound drawing tablet to use as a science notebook. For the stream-table data collection, Amy provided a simple diagram of the stream table divided into quadrants to guide their observational drawing, but she left all other decisions about how to record data to the students.

Erin's notebook entries provide a chronological sequence of the work. The detail in the drawings along with annotations and labels help the reader know what Erin observed. Her entries demonstrate understanding of the investigation question and her language use is varied with scientific terms used appropriately. There are multiple examples of evidence of reasoning (prior experience, explanations), and she is clear about the difference between experience and evidence from classroom activities. Erin has also crafted a clear and complete conclusion that pulls together all the activities and includes (1) reference to the investigation question, (2) a claim, and (3) evidence and experiences to support the claim. She has chosen to present her conclusion spatially to show the relationship between the many pieces of information she presents.

Although Erin includes many important elements of science notebooks, the entries do not have headings or introductions that explain their place in the investigation sequence. The purpose of the activity or the question being pursued is assumed and not made explicit. In all likelihood, a simple reminder from Amy would solve this problem. Erin does need to work on thinking through predictions and their role in an investigation. One appears above the drawings of the sedimentation jars (dated 5/5), but she does not refer to it after sedimentation has occurred. Amy might choose to spend time with Erin, or indeed the whole class, discussing the importance of making thoughtful predictions and providing reasons for them.

Using your experince, what   5/2
evidence can you think of that
supports the idea that flowing
water changes the surface of land?

Evidence

- The pressure of the water pushes on the sand.

- The current may make a certain pattern or the way the water flows.

- The design it usually makes of pattern is mini up and down hills which is alot like the flowing water pattern.

- Flowing water can dissolve stuff as well which might make something look different. Sometimes how big the body of water is effects the water flowing and its pattern.

ERIN'S NOTEBOOK page 1

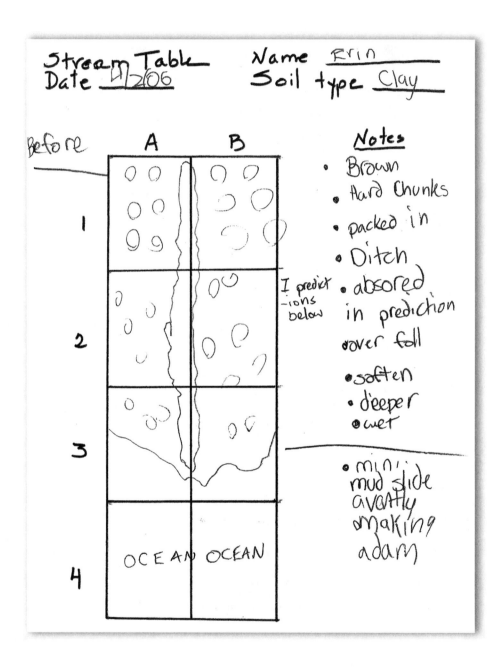

ERIN'S NOTEBOOK page 2

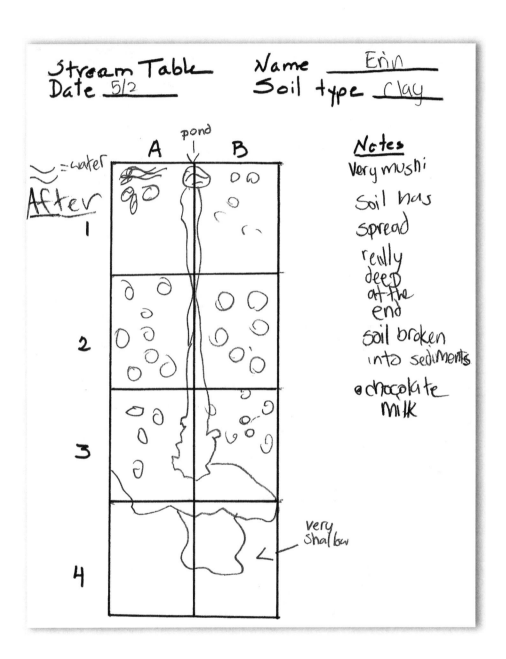

Stream Table   Name ___Erin___
Date _5/2___   Soil type __Clay__

pond

A   B

~ = water

After

1

2

3

4

very
shallow

Notes
Very mushi

Soil has
spread

really
deep
at the
end

soil broken
into sediments

• chocolate
milk

ERIN'S NOTEBOOK page 3

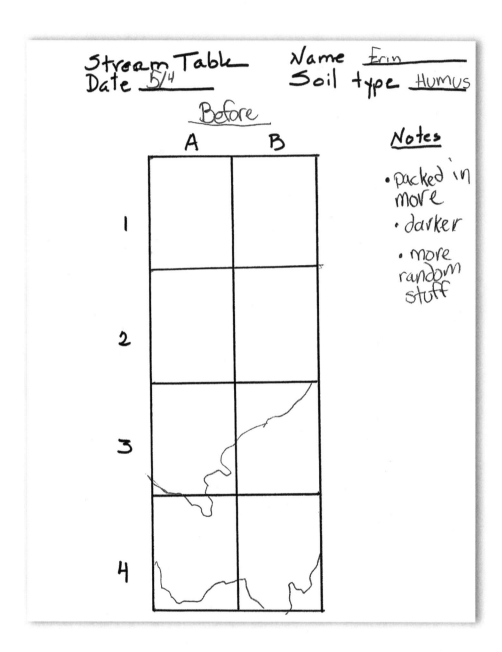

Stream Table   Name Erin
Date 5/4   Soil type Humus

Before

	A	B
1		
2		
3		
4		

Notes

- packed in more
- darker
- more random stuff

ERIN'S NOTEBOOK page 4

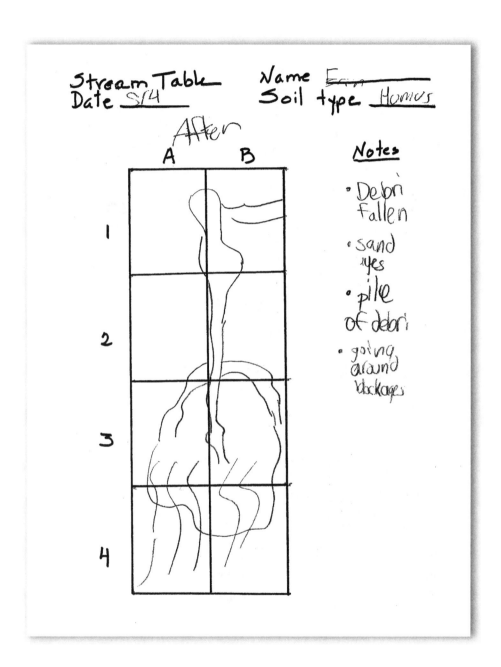

Stream Table　Name E___
Date _S/4_　Soil type _Humus_

After

A　B

Notes

- Debri
  Fallen

- sand
  yes

- pile
  of debri

- going
  around
  blockages

1

2

3

4

ERIN'S NOTEBOOK　page 5

Clay	HS	SS
Brown	Dark Brown	yellow
M packed	Dark ?	grains
chunchs	hard rough	bumpy
smooth + Bumpy		

Sandy soil is weak and water flows any way it wants.

Humus soil is hard and water changes direction when it is blocked.

Clay soil works it's way and does not pay attention to changing direction and if it does it is only a little bit.

	Sandy Tan	Clay	Humus
color	Yelbw/Brown	Light Brown	Dark Bram
part	Grains of Minerals+Rocks		minerals
tex	bumpy	Clumps	clumps/bum-py
hard soft	Soft	Soft	really soft / pack-ed in
i m	bits of things		pumpkin roots seeds twiggs

ERIN'S NOTEBOOK page 6

5/5

Lighter stuff will flow to the surface
and the soil will sink and otufc
will go on top. Water will fill
the rest. Sandy grains may go
to the top. Same will happen
in each enless there is sandy
soil. <u>Prediction</u> Big Chunks

will sink imedditly

| CLAY | HUMUS | SANDY | Miystear |

Clay=
De-Eafe

Humus=
Coffee

Sandy=
tea leaves

Myster=
? ? ?

ERIN'S NOTEBOOK page 7

5/9

After

Mix   Hum   Clay   Sand

The soil sinks into layers and
after a long period of time it
would turn into sedimentery rock.
Some water evaperated and is putting
pressure on the soil.

ERIN'S NOTEBOOK page 8

5/12

Using your experince, what evidence can you think of that supports the idea that flowing water changes the surface of land

Evidence

- I saw it pushing away bits of rock and rock is part of land stream tables
- When the water is flowing fast and hard it pushes down on the ground and starts sink -ing into the ground
  - stream tables
- When water flows it gathers or picks of things then when it settle it will evend -uly in a very very long time turn into sedimen -tary rock.
  - Sedimentary bottles
- rocks can change into + different things wron they are eroded - Granite + sand

Experinces

- stream tables putting different soils in and obser -er the water flowing into th ocean.
- sediment bottles shaking up different soils and obser -ing them settle.
- Granite and sand Studing the granite and taking notes then with the sand. Then we looked at there similaritys. Mica, feldspar and quarts. They had the same minerals.

This is why flowing water can change the surface of the land. I can show you on the left my **Evidence** and my **Experince** of the experiments about how flowing water can change the surface of the land.

ERIN'S NOTEBOOK page 9

▶ For Further Reading

Aschbacher, Pamela R., and Alicia C. Alonzo. 2004. Using Science Notebooks to Assess Students' Conceptual Understanding. Paper presented at the annual meeting of the American Educational Research Association, 12–16 April, San Diego.

This paper discusses the use of science notebooks as an assessment tool and whether their use improves instruction or student achievement. Findings suggest that notebooks can be highly valuable depending on the teacher's pedagogical approach, content knowledge, and general understanding of both formative and summative assessment.

Baxter, Gail P., Kristen M. Bass, and Robert Glaser. 2000. *CSE Technical Report: An Analysis of Notebook Writing in Elementary Science Classrooms*. Los Angeles: National Center for Research on Evaluation, CRESST/CSE, Graduate School of Education and Information Studies, University of California, Los Angeles.

This study examined teacher practice and the teacher's role in facilitating student use of notebooks in order to determine how well notebook use can monitor both teaching and learning. Findings indicated that students recorded procedures and results in their notebooks, accurately reflecting teachers' instructions, but did not use the notebooks to describe their thinking, reasoning, or hypotheses.

Fulton, Lori, and Brian Campbell. 2002. *Science Notebooks: Writing About Inquiry*. Portsmouth, NH: Heinemann.

This book is a primer for setting up and using science notebooks in elementary classrooms. The authors relate their experiences of years of investigating the use of science notebooks by students, teachers, and practicing scientists. It includes classroom vignettes and student notebook entries from different grade levels.

———. 2004. "Student-Centered Notebooks." *Science and Children* 42 (3): 26–29.

This article offers guidelines for developing and using student-centered notebooks. The authors argue that students are more likely to use their notebooks effectively (for recording their understandings and reasoning) if they are given ownership; when teachers maintain control, students tend to write what they think their teachers want to see. The authors offer useful strategies to help teachers adeptly facilitate the use of student science notebooks.

Fulwiler, Betsy Rupp. 2007. *Writing in Science: How to Scaffold Instruction to Support Learning*. Portsmouth, NH: Heinemann.

Writing in Science describes the Expository Writing and Science Notebooks Program that has been at work for the better part of a decade in the Seattle,

Washington, public schools. It is a very accessible, practical guide for teachers wishing to move students beyond recounting what they did to writing about their thinking. This book shares strategies the program has found successful in many classrooms and includes a number of examples of student science writing.

Klentschy, Michael P. 2008. *Using Science Notebooks in Elementary Classrooms*. Arlington, VA: NSTA Press.

This book is a practical guide for implementing science notebooks. The author, a former school superintendent who implemented district-wide elementary science notebooks, discusses research-based best practices such as scaffolds, sentence starters, and writing prompts. The book addresses how notebooks increase language fluency and writing proficiency and how science notebooks can be used as an effective assessment tool.

Ruiz-Primo, Maria Araceli, Min Li, and Richard J. Shavelson. 2001. Looking into Students' Science Notebooks: What Do Teachers Do with Them? Paper presented at the annual meeting of the American Educational Research Association, 10–14 April, Seattle.

This paper reports on a study of the use of students' science notebooks to examine teachers' instruction in science classrooms. In analyzing the notebooks, the authors considered the characteristics of instructional activities, quality of student performance, and teacher feedback. The findings showed that the instructional activities were not intellectually challenging, often asking students to record the results of an experiment or copy definitions; teachers provided very little feedback; and students' skills and understanding did not improve.

CHAPTER 8 | Science Writing: Beyond the Notebook

When you are doing the research yourself you are using your own words to describe what you see and it's easier to understand. You don't have to worry about making someone else's words your own. I feel like I really learned something about chicks from watching them every day.

—A FIFTH GRADER, ASKED TO COMMENT ON HIS EXPERIENCE WITH WRITING ABOUT HIS STUDY OF CHICKS

Writing is an important component of science learning at every stage of the inquiry process. As described in the previous chapter, students write in their science notebooks throughout an inquiry, just as scientists do to create a clear, complete, and chronological record of their work. Students also write reflections about their work in their notebooks, and as an inquiry comes to a close, they write their conclusions. But the notebook with these varied entries is not the only kind of writing scientists do. They also communicate with their colleagues and the public. It is this form of communication that is the focus of this chapter.

Within the science community, scientists open the door to discussion and debate concerning their procedures, interpretation of data, and conclusions through publishing articles that describe their work. A scientist might publish a scientific report in a journal. She might be asked to write an article about her work for a newspaper or be an expert witness in a trial. In each case, the audience and purpose of the piece of writing guide the scientist's choice of language, writing style, and structure for framing ideas. But whether a scientific journal article, newspaper column, or legal brief, the writing springs from the same scientific work carefully documented in notebook entries.

Similarly, in the classroom, student notebooks contain the raw material for other kinds of writing. Just as scientists write to engage their scientific peers and the public in discussion, in debate, and in an exchange of ideas about their work, so can students. At the upper-elementary level, this might take the form of a feature article on electric circuits for the school newspaper, a how-to guide for the class down the hall about launching a study of butterfly life cycles, an autobiographical account of hatching chicks, or a letter to the school board concerning erosion in the school yard. Here, students are communicating with a variety of audiences about their investigations, what they have learned from a unit of study, or an application of their learning to an immediate problem.

This kind of writing takes place at the end of a unit and relies heavily on the investigations done by the students and the records they have kept in their science notebooks. Their own investigations are at the heart of their work and become the basis for their writing: both the data they have collected and analyzed and their ideas, reflections, and conclusions. As they review their notebooks for content, students may also discover gaps in their recording, entries that are illegible, and conclusions that are incomplete. This is a strong motivation to identify and set goals for improving those entries in the future. It also can guide the teacher in identifying skills that need to be taught.

— makes them review their entries.

The process of writing for a broader audience—people who were not present during the investigation—helps students clarify and deepen their understanding of the science concepts in a number of ways. They need to review their questions and ideas, synthesize the ideas they are grappling with, and generalize their knowledge. They also need to identify areas of confusion or lingering questions and possibly do research using secondary sources including books, articles, and the Internet, to add to their understanding. Finally, they need to apply their understanding in a new and different context and practice clear and effective communication of science ideas. From a literacy learning perspective, science writing provides wonderful opportunities for students to apply in an authentic context the literacy skills and strategies they have learned. In many ways, this kind of science writing represents the ultimate connection between science and literacy.

Writing in this way is different from what happens already in many classrooms where science research reports are assigned to help students develop research skills, gather information, and write reports about a single topic, such as endangered species, the rain forest, or dinosaurs. For these reports, students use only secondary sources. They read about the assigned topic, capture the ideas of others, and restate the information in their own words. This kind of writing asks students to do a limited amount of scientific thinking and reasoning as they process information; hence, the teaching focuses more on the craft of presenting information about the topic in a clear and interesting way and less on developing a deeper understanding of the science concept. There is a place for this type of writing, but it is not the focus of this chapter.

> *The writing that we did during the science unit is different from research-based nonfiction writing in the writing workshop. It was more similar to when we wrote feature articles. A lot of the children did surveys or interviews, and it was a struggle for them to take those interviews and survey questions and write a feature article that made sense and proved their angles. That was a connection that we found to the science writing. You have this data and how do you craft it in a way that makes sense for your reader? It's almost easier to take someone else's ideas and write about them than it is to write about your own. I think it's also hard for them to value their own notebook as much as a published text on a topic. It's harder for students to trust what they've done.*

It's easy to trust someone else who wrote something and it's got a fancy cover and it was edited and published, so they must be right.

—KIRSTEN SHROUT, TEACHER, PERSONAL INTERVIEW

▌ Writing Genres

There are many nonfiction genres of writing from which students can draw when they write about their science work, including nonfiction narrative, persuasive writing, instructional writing, and the formal report. While writing fiction can be a vehicle for presenting science learning, elementary students typically have various opportunities for this type of writing but few, if any, opportunities to use empirical evidence to write analytically, scientifically, and persuasively or to write nonfiction narrative. Science provides opportunities for teachers to make the less common forms of nonfiction writing appealing and authentic and provides students with opportunities to practice a different set of important skills.

As we got closer to wrapping up the unit, we asked as writers, "How can we grow our ideas into a published piece?" I was nervous because I thought, "They're not going to know what they could create from their observations and their evidence in their notebook." But when I posed the question to them, they came up with this long list that I couldn't even have imagined. We had how-tos, and directions, and all-abouts. We had some students say, "Oh, my autobiography or my memoir of my life as a scientist or my growth as a scientist." And some kids were saying, "Oh, I could write a graphic novel and through the story I could, you know, teach people what I've learned." I was really impressed with how they took everything that they've been exposed to as writers. For me, it didn't seem so easy to transfer, but for them it was just "Oh, of course we can write this and make these things."

—KIRSTEN SHROUT, TEACHER, PERSONAL INTERVIEW

Each writing genre has different characteristics and specific structures and calls on students to apply the knowledge and experience they have gained through their primary investigations and some secondary sources in a different way. For example, in one fifth-grade classroom studying crayfish, a student chose to write an instructional piece about the importance of establishing an appropriate classroom habitat for crayfish if they are to survive. Drawing from his experience, he described some of their needs, their natural habitat, and how his class tried to replicate these conditions in the classroom. He also went to the Internet and included some of the ways in which the environments of crayfish are being damaged and how these factors can be avoided in the artificial classroom habitat. For this writing, the student drew first on his direct experience instead of writing only about something he learned from the Internet.

In another classroom, at the end of a unit on electrical circuits, several students decided to write a how-to book on electric things. One student described how to make a flashlight using the knowledge he had gained about electrical circuits to explain what was important to think about.

Two examples of final drafts of writing from direct experience are included below. They come from Amy Flax's fourth-grade classroom, where students spent several weeks investigating the life cycles of insects, including the mealworm beetle (Tenebrio)

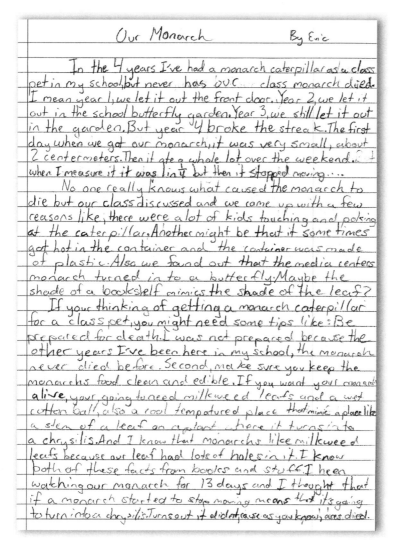

STUDENT WRITING ABOUT THE MONARCH BUTTERFLY: Eric

and monarch and painted lady butterflies. The students documented their observations through drawings and notes in their science notebooks. At one point, their monarch pupa died. This experience led several students to decide to write how-to chapters for a classroom down the hall that was soon to be studying the monarch life cycle. Amy provided time in the writing block for the students to work through their drafts, revisions, and final edits.

Tips for the Classroom

If you get insects in your classroom, there are things you should pay attention to. If I were the teacher I would have my kids observe the insects. They should watch every day and write down what they see in their notebooks.

Here are my tips.

The larva is the caterpillar or worm. The teacher has to check the cotton ball or sponge, or whatever it drinks from to see if it's moist everyday. And check if it has a fresh food source. It's important to do this because the insect won't eat dried up food. And it needs fresh food everyday.

A pupa for the monarch is when the caterpillar has made himself into a cocoon. A pupa for the mealworm looks different and dead. When the insect is in the pupa stage I would have adults back there because they are very delicate animals. I never took my mealworm out of its cage in the pupa stage. They are VERY delicate in the pupa stage.

I would not have my kids touch it because our hands have oils on them. I know this because when I went to Pennsylvania I went to caves and we weren't allowed to touch the rocks because our hands have oils on them. So I was thinking that it would infect or hurt the insect. In our classroom we touched the monarch and it died after that. Maybe that might be why the monarch died. But another way the monarch might have died is it might not have got fresh food. All the time.

The tips that you have just learned come from a student that had 3 different insects in her classroom—A mealworm a monarch, and a painted lady. Having insects in her classroom isn't as simple as it seems. After watching them over the past month I realized that insects need the same amount of care as you do!

STUDENT WRITING ABOUT THE MONARCH BUTTERFLY: Annie

Some Guidelines for Science Writing

The Importance of Firsthand Experiences

To write in the way just described, students must

- conduct science investigations of at least several weeks' duration

- gather and record data in notebooks

- analyze data

- make claims based on their evidence

- synthesize their specific claims to come to a more general understanding of the focus concepts of the unit

If these conditions are in place, students' writing can have a number of purposes, address different audiences, and take many forms depending on student interests, what they have learned about writing, talk, and research in literacy, and the combined literacy and science goals of the class. In reports, factual accounts, articles to the school newspaper, letters, or proposals to a local business, students may present and defend their work, choose to persuade or take a stance, or describe something they have done. The choice of genre and audience is less important than the opportunity to use their knowledge and experience to communicate with a wider audience.

Facilitating Science Writing

Writing in science as in other areas needs to be taught explicitly and modeled if students are to be successful. Many of the instructional strategies used in a literacy program can be applied to science writing. If students have learned the basics of certain genres in their literacy work, they can bring these skills and strategies to their science writing. However, regardless of how much they have learned through the literacy program, they will also need explicit instruction and resources as they use these skills in science. They will need to

- see models of various kinds of science writing

- have access to a rich array of trade books for independent reading

- participate in interactive read-alouds using an array of texts

- have access to content vocabulary they have learned and reminders that using science vocabulary accurately is important

- learn through direct instruction and modeling how to use their notebooks as sources of data, evidence, ideas, and explanations

The ultimate goal, of course, is to communicate clear and accurate science ideas to various audiences in a variety of ways.

▶ Conclusion

I saw one of my students really improve in writing. She really had an interest in plants. She liked being able to make observations, talk about the observations, share ideas with others, and build ideas from others. For her, because of her multiple opportunities to visualize, experiment, and talk about it, it really, really enhanced her writing. If it's just a writers' workshop session where students have to write, the first sentence is hard to come by sometimes and the second sentence and the third sentence. But having an experience gives you something to talk about and to write about, and she had a lot to write about.

—SHARON SEALY, TEACHER, PERSONAL INTERVIEW

Inquiry-based science provides an authentic context for student writing. When they use their own data gathered in investigations and recorded in notebooks as the basis for some of the writing taught in the writing program, students have ownership of the process and content. When students write about their firsthand investigations, they are making choices about genre, audience, what information to include, and how to articulate their thinking. Simultaneously, they deepen their knowledge of science and enhance their skills as writers.

▶ For Further Reading

Gunel, Murat, Brian Hand, and Vaughan Prain. 2007. "Writing for Learning in Science: A Secondary Analysis of Six Studies." *International Journal of Science and Mathematics Education* 5 (4): 615–37.

This article reports on a secondary analysis of six studies that were part of a larger research program about the use of writing-to-learn strategies in science. When compared with students using traditional writing strategies, the achievement of students using the writing-to-learn strategies was significantly higher. The authors contend that traditional writing strategies encourage students to simply repeat what they have learned, whereas writing-to-learn strategies promote re-representation of knowledge, affording students greater opportunities to learn.

Tower, Cathy. 2005. "What's the Purpose? Students Talk About Writing in Science." *Language Arts* 82 (6): 472–83.

This article describes a study of students' understanding about their reasons for writing in science. In looking at student interviews, three issues emerged:

purpose, audience, and use of visuals. In further discussing these themes, the author notes that student answers often echoed ideas communicated by the teacher. Suggestions are given for providing students with authentic writing experiences so they can learn to communicate effectively.

Wallace, Carolyn S., Brian Hand, and Vaughan Prain. 2007. *Writing and Learning in the Science Classroom*. New York: Springer.

This book offers evidence to support the authors' contention that writing does improve science learning. The authors provide a comprehensive review of salient literature in the field and detailed reports of their own research studies. They also suggest current and future issues concerning writing in science.

Afterword

This book is one of two products of a National Science Foundation project called Connecting Science and Literacy: Professional Development Resources for Teachers in the Upper Elementary Classroom. The other product is a guide for professional development leaders. This book was written to spark dialogue among educators and to be a catalyst for developing new approaches and strategies in the teaching of inquiry-based science.

Our intent was to uncover some of the important components of the science and literacy connection as they are or could be implemented in the classroom and to share these as well as selected instructional strategies with educators. It was not to develop a specific instructional guide or methodology. The book draws from many sources, not the least of which is the practice and thinking of a group of teachers who were members of the development team and whose words are quoted throughout the book. As part of the development work, we spent many hours in their classrooms to learn important aspects of their practice from them and their students. The book also draws from professional developers and teachers who piloted, field-tested, and critiqued our ideas.

Working closely with professionals in the field also helped us clarify the challenges and, in some cases, the barriers many teachers face as they attempt to develop their science programs and include not only direct experience but more discussion and writing about ideas. It was important that our products would guide practitioners toward new and innovative practice but also reflect the realities of their professional lives. We learned a number of things that are important to share at the end of this book, in part because they acknowledge the context in which teachers do their work and in part to encourage teachers and those who work with teachers to work together to meet the challenges and eliminate the barriers.

All the teachers with whom we worked were already engaging their students in direct experiences. If students are to talk and write about their science work, direct experience is critical and is in itself a challenge in many classrooms where time, space, materials, and curricula are not easily available. Many teachers used books with a science focus to provide students with opportunities to read nonfiction and, in particular, informational books. Many also used a variety of worksheets and/or science journals in their science teaching and held group question-and-answer sessions about the science content.

The challenge for all was to move beyond these practices to a deeper understanding of the role of literacy in science and new ways of making the connections. For many, this meant developing a deeper understanding of scientific inquiry and how to rethink the balance between coverage of a body of content and providing opportunities for students to engage in science inquiry. This was hard not only because of a prevailing view of science as content but also because of the breadth of content to be covered in many state and district frameworks and tests that emphasize content.

Another challenge was to think through the balance between the hands-on activities and time spent thinking, talking, and writing about ideas. In many classrooms, if indeed hands-on science activities take place, the time available does not allow for the important thinking and reasoning processes. In some cases, we found ourselves suggesting less time for the hands-on part of science inquiry and more time for the thinking and communicating.

Yet another challenge for the teachers was to adapt the instructional strategies they were using in literacy to the demands of science. It was not as natural a process as one might think. For example, as our work proceeded, it became increasingly clear that a major stumbling block for many teachers and students was the structure of science discussions. Contrary to what many of them did in literacy and even in mathematics, the science discussions were dominated by teacher talk and had a traditional initiate-respond-evaluate format in which the teacher asked a question, one student responded, and the teacher evaluated the answer as right or wrong.

Facilitating discussions that encouraged student-to-student interaction proved difficult. One of the development teachers started by simply pulling herself out of the circle and telling the students she would no longer contribute to their discussions; they would need to proceed without her. Another teacher started taking notes during the discussion, which encouraged her to listen more carefully and kept her from intervening as frequently. Over time, these strategies, coupled with direct instruction, significantly changed the nature of the science discussions in these teachers' classrooms.

Two other challenges emerged from this focus on science talk. As students began to share and debate ideas, the teachers realized they needed to be very clear about the science concepts the unit of study was focused on. They also needed to understand the science quite deeply to be able to keep students focused and guide them toward appropriate conclusions. And they needed to learn to craft a good discussion question that would engage and challenge student thinking about the science concepts.

Another difficulty for many teachers was moving from whatever form of worksheets, notebooks, and journals they were using to an authentic science notebook. This required rethinking the role of science notebooks and the critical components. In some cases, it meant giving up expectations of neatness and grammatical correctness and taking on the significant challenge of developing students' skill in drawing conclusions from their work.

Regardless of which challenge or challenges individual teachers faced, they realized that changing the role of literacy in science involved new skills for them and for their students. They needed to use new instructional strategies and their students needed to learn new skills through explicit instruction in how to discuss science concepts, keep a science notebook, and write about their science ideas. They needed instruction in the similarities and differences between what they did in literacy and what was expected of them in science.

A major challenge for all, not related to new skills or strategies, was to find the time for significant science in the weekly schedule—to provide time for students to read, write, and talk about science as well as conduct hands-on investigations. Our new emphasis on talking and writing in science, coupled with the necessity for hands-on work, meant that science would take more time. The key was to see that "extra" time as benefiting not only the learning of science but also student skills in literacy. For this to happen, for science and literacy to share some time, there had to be active support from the school administrator as well as other curriculum support staff. In one classroom in a school with such support, writing in science notebooks and writing about science became part of the writing block.

Despite all of these challenges, the professionals with whom we have worked have been unanimous in their enthusiasm for the steps they have taken in their classrooms and the accomplishments of their students. It is clear from these teachers that developing the role of literacy in science provides opportunities for students to think more deeply about science ideas through discussion and writing and, in the process, refine their scientific reasoning skills and many literacy practices.

It is fitting to end this book with the words that a few of our teacher colleagues offered when asked about their experiences in bringing talk and writing into their science teaching in new ways.

> *I was blown away by how much the children loved to write in science in this format. And we had done science reports on Earth forces many months prior. That was fun for them, but there was some type of spark that was missing that I noticed in this type of writing—writing about the worms and writing about our experiments. I think that probably came from the fact that they chose the experiment they wanted in terms of which types of soil to use to see what the worms preferred. They had had this delightful inspiring conversation before the experience even began.*
>
> *A big aha moment for me was how clearly science notebooks emboldened and strengthened children's confidence, enabling them to put out ideas that they would not necessarily have wanted to talk about in science prior to this experience. I felt that most of my children participated in some ways, whether through lots of writing or lots of conversation or discussion in their small groups—they all had ideas.*
>
> —RACHEL KRAMER, TEACHER, PERSONAL INTERVIEW

> *So, [a science notebook is] an unbelievably powerful tool. It really is. And it's something that I'll never not do now because I think it takes their understanding and it gives meaning to what they're doing in a way that wasn't going on before the use of*

notebooks. And I think ultimately that whether it's in science or in literacy, what we're trying to help kids with is to find meaning, and this is remarkable for that.

I think in the past there wasn't as much accountability. We would do experiments. We might write about it once or we might discuss it once. But by going through what is really a lengthy but worthwhile and better process of an inquiry where you're spending time, . . . in the end, it's more significant and meaningful for the kids.
—AMY FLAX, TEACHER, PERSONAL INTERVIEW

Many teachers may not feel persuaded . . . , but I think once they started to use [discussions and notebooks], they would immediately see the benefits, and kids—it just seems to me like the more that we've used the notebooks and had the science talks, that kids are getting [a] better understanding of the science, that it's forcing them to be responsible for what they learned in science, and giving them the opportunities to ask more questions, to look back at what they did, to recognize how they've learned.
—SUZANNE NORTON, TEACHER, PERSONAL INTERVIEW

Study Guide

▶ Introduction

The chapters in this book can be used in a variety of settings as the focus for discussion and reflection. One such setting is the teacher study group. Almost always based in a school and focused on common interests, study groups are important vehicles for professional development. There exist many sets of guidelines for implementing teacher study groups, and this overview is not meant to be all-inclusive. Rather, what follows are some brief guidelines for setting up a study group and a set of suggested questions for each part of the book as well as for each chapter.

▶ Study Groups

Organizing a Study Group

Organizing a study group can be viewed as a set of basic steps.

1. Form the study group around a topic of inquiry.

Study groups are generally most effective if the number of participants does not exceed eight and if there is a skilled facilitator (see p. 101). The facilitator might be a teacher leader, curriculum leader, or science or literacy coach. Once a facilitator is identified, the next step is to identify a focus of study—the topic. A group might focus on one of the parts of the book or on one or two of the chapters for a more in-depth study.

2. Develop focus questions that will guide the work of the study group.

Given a focus for the study group, the next step is to identify two or three key questions. The objective of a study group is to provide an opportunity for a group of teachers to deepen their understanding of an aspect of their teaching and to enhance their skills through close analysis of their classroom practice. Too broad a focus defeats the objective; too narrow a focus may not spark rich dialogue. Following this overview of study groups are lists of questions for consideration. These are, of course, only suggestions. The specific context and interests of study group members will play a large role in determining the key questions.

3. Design the action plan.

With a topic and a few initial questions identified, the members of the study group should now establish basic operating guidelines. Following are some important guidelines to set:

- the norms of discussion that the group will follow and some basic expectations (see "Norms and Expectations for Study Groups" below)

- the nature of the specific tasks or actions the group will take between study group meetings (e.g., reading, classroom implementation, collection of student work to share and analyze)

- who will record at each session

- the basic session protocol

In addition, it is critical to develop an overall plan for the work of the study group and a tentative action plan for each session, including some key discussion points and the tasks to be accomplished. While a hallmark of study group work is the flexibility to pursue issues that come up and to take on challenges as they are identified, it is critical to have a basic structure in place. This plan serves as a starting point and can be modified once the study group is under way.

4. Determine what, if any, other resources beyond the readings will be gathered.

The chapters in this book are the core of the study group; however, an action plan may go beyond these. For example, if notebooks are the focus of a group, there are a number of new books and articles on science notebooks that might be useful. If the study group members are practicing teachers, the experience is likely to be much richer if the discussion of ideas in the book is connected with participants' classroom practice and the sharing of student work, classroom video, or other artifacts.

Norms and Expectations for Study Groups

In successful study groups, participants develop a set of group norms and expectations to which they all agree. The group may want to post and revisit these expectations at each study group session and to make changes as needed. While it may seem unnecessary to state these explicitly, experience suggests that the crafting of the list and regular review are important to establishing a culture in which challenging and productive study can take place. Following is an example of such a list.

Study Group Norms and Expectations

- Come regularly and on time.

- Do any assignments for the session.

- Come prepared to share thinking and ideas and discuss the agreed-upon topic.

- Bring any artifacts and examples to discuss.

- Sit in a circle around a table.

- Understand the purpose of the study group, study group format, and norms and expectations for discussion.

- Stay on focus.

- Agree to disagree respectfully.

- Encourage one another to challenge ideas and to have different opinions.

The Facilitator

Study groups are made up of peers; however, they function most productively when there is a designated facilitator. The role of the facilitator is to create a group dynamic where members feel comfortable taking an active role. The facilitator is not in the role of the expert. If the group treats her as an expert or she assumes this role, the study group will become more like a workshop or seminar and be less likely to accomplish its objectives. At the start, the facilitator will probably need to guide the group more strongly, supporting the norms and expectations, keeping the focus clear, and helping establish a culture of collective collaboration. But over time, as the norms are established and the group develops its own learning identity, the facilitator will release responsibility to the group.

Facilitator tasks include

- helping the group adhere to norms for discussion and expectations for participation

- supporting the recorder in documenting the session and keeping facilitation notes for herself (e.g., resources that might have been useful, issues with group dynamics, and new questions that were raised)

- making sure participants leave with tasks to be accomplished and the place and date of the next session

- making sure any needed resources are collected for each of the study group sessions

Documentation of the Work of the Study Group

Documenting the ongoing study group work encourages reflection and synthesis of the ideas discussed at each session. Recording the key points, questions, predictions, and ideas over time provides evidence of a learning trajectory and helps study group members see the progress of their thinking.

The documentation of the sessions ultimately becomes the story of the study group's work. It is advisable to have a structure or template for the recorder so that the documentation is consistent and includes important elements of each session. These forms can be filled in and sent out to all members immediately following each session. They also are kept by the facilitator along with other study group artifacts.

▶ Key Questions

SECTION ONE   Essentials

General Questions

- According to your experience and the reading, what are some connections between science and literacy?

- What are some similarities in the approach to teaching and learning between inquiry science and balanced literacy?

- How does inquiry-based science with strong literacy connections support diverse learners?

- What are the benefits to student science learning when there are many opportunities to talk and write?

- What are the benefits to student literacy learning when students talk and write in science?

Chapter Questions

Science Inquiry

- Based on your experience and the reading, how would you define science inquiry?

- What are some of the benefits for students' science learning when they engage in inquiry?

- In what ways is science in your classroom inquiry based? How might you increase the opportunities for students to engage in science inquiry?

- What challenges do you face in implementing science inquiry in your classroom? How might you overcome them?

Balanced Literacy and Science Inquiry

- Based on your experience and the reading, what do you think are important elements of balanced literacy?

- In what ways do you incorporate some or all of these elements into your classroom practice?

- What instructional strategies from literacy do you use in your science teaching?

- What literacy skills and strategies do your students use in their science work?

Teacher Questions That Support Inquiry

- Based on your experience and the reading, what do you think makes a question productive?

- To what extent do you ask productive questions? What are some examples?

- What strategies might you use to improve your questioning?

Science Inquiry and English Language Learners

- According to your experience and the reading, what instructional strategies support ELLs in the science classroom?

- In what ways do support strategies for ELL students benefit the learning of all students?

- What support strategies do you use in different areas of the curriculum? In science?

SECTION TWO   The Role of Talk in Science Inquiry

General Questions

- Based on your experience and the reading, what do you think is the role of talk in learning science?

- How do whole-group discussions support students' science learning?

- What skills and strategies do you and your students need to learn for effective whole-group discussions?

- What challenges do you face in implementing whole-group science discussions? How might you overcome these?

- How do talk and writing interact in science teaching and learning?

Chapter Questions

A Culture of Talk

- Based on your experience and the reading, what do you think characterizes a culture of talk in the classroom?

- Two strategies are highlighted in the chapter: the circle and wait time. How do these contribute to the effectiveness of whole-group discussion? How might you implement these strategies in your classroom?

- What norms and expectations do you have in your classroom, how were they established, and how do they support effective discussion?

- To what extent do students talk with one another in discussions? What strategies might you use to increase their interaction?

- How do you or might you engage the more reluctant speakers?

- In what ways are the discussion skills and strategies students use in literacy and in science the same or different?

Classroom Talk: Gathering-Ideas and Making-Meaning Discussions

- Based on your experience and the reading, what do you think are some important characteristics of group discussions that take place during each of the four stages of inquiry?

- How would you compare and contrast the purposes and the characteristics of gathering-ideas discussions and making-meaning discussions?

- What are some facilitation strategies you use or might use at each stage of inquiry? How and why are they different? How are they the same?

- What scientific reasoning skills are students developing through their discussions at different stages of inquiry?

- In what ways are discussions that take place during literacy the same as discussions that take place in science? How are they different?

SECTION THREE   Writing in Science

General Questions

- According to your experience and the reading, why is it important to write in science?

- What challenges have you experienced in getting students to write in science? How might you overcome these?

- What instructional strategies that you use in writing might you use in teaching science writing? How do writing skills you teach in literacy transfer to writing in science?

- How do talk and writing interact in science teaching and learning?

- In what ways does writing in science develop students' literacy skills as well as their science understanding?

Chapter Questions

The Science Notebook

- According to your experience and the reading, what is the role of the science notebook in science learning and what are some essential characteristics of the science notebook?

- How do students learn the skills and understanding they need to keep effective science notebooks?

- In what ways can you make the use of science notebooks authentic?

- Writing reflections and developing conclusions can be very challenging to students. What science reasoning and writing skills do students need to learn to be successful? What are some instructional strategies you could use?

- How do you provide feedback to students about the recording they are doing in their notebooks? Why is it important?

Science Writing: Beyond the Notebook

- Based on your experience and the reading, how do you think writing beyond the notebook enhances students' science learning?

- What are the benefits and drawbacks for science learning of writing from direct experience and of writing from secondary sources?

- What do you see as an appropriate balance among different approaches to science writing?

- How might you make a connection between your writing program and the writing students do in science?

References

Black, Paul, and Dylan Wiliam. 1998. "Inside the Black Box: Raising Standards Through Classroom Assessment." *Phi Delta Kappan* 80 (2): 139–48.

Bloem, Patricia L. 2004. "Correspondence Journals: Talk That Matters." *The Reading Teacher* 58 (1): 54–62.

Bransford, J. D., A. L. Brown, and R. R. Cocking. 1999. *How People Learn*. Washington, DC: National Academies Press.

Douglas, Rowena, Michael P. Klentschy, Karen Worth, and Wendy Binder. 2006. *Linking Science and Literacy in the K–8 Classroom*. Arlington, VA: National Science Teachers Association.

Elstgeest, Jos. 2001. "The Right Question at the Right Time." In *Primary Science: Taking the Plunge*, 2d. ed, Wynne Harlen: 25–34. Portsmouth, NH: Heinemann.

Fletcher, Ralph. 1996. *A Writer's Notebook: Unlocking the Writer Within You*. New York: HarperTrophy.

Fulwiler, Betsy Rupp. 2007. *Writing in Science: How to Scaffold Instruction to Support Learning*. Portsmouth, NH: Heinemann.

Harlen, Wynne. 2005. *Teaching, Learning and Assessing Science 5–12*. 4th ed. London: Sage.

Lee, Okhee. (n.d.) Integrating Content Areas with English Language Development for English Language Learners [white paper]. Retrieved from Glencoe Research: http://www.glencoe.com/glencoe_research/Math/icawp.pdf

Michaels, Sarah, Andrew W. Shouse, and Heidi A. Schweingruber. 2007. *Ready, Set, Science! Putting Research to Work in K–8 Science Classrooms*. Washington, DC: National Academies Press.

National Research Council. 1996. *National Science Education Standards*. Washington, DC: National Academy Press.

———. 2007. *Taking Science to School: Learning and Teaching Science in Grades K–8*. Washington, DC: National Academies Press.

Pearson, David, Laura R. Roehler, Janice A. Dole, and Gerald G. Duffy. 1992. "Developing Expertise in Reading Comprehension." In *What Research Has to Say About Reading Instruction*, 2d ed., ed. S. Jay Samuels and Alan Farstrup: 145–99. Newark, DE: International Reading Association.

Pine, Jerome. 1996. The Science Notebook. Unpublished paper.

Resnick, Lauren B. 1999. "Making America Smarter." *Education Week Century Series* 18 (40): 38–40.

Vygotsky, Lev V. 1934. *Thought and Language*. Moscow-Leningrad: Sokegiz.

Zimmermann, Susan, and Ellin Keene. 2007. *Mosaic of Thought: The Power of Comprehension Strategy Instruction*. 2d ed. Portsmouth, NH: Heinemann.